BOUNDLESS:

Your How-To Guide to Practical Remote Viewing

LORI LAMBERT WILLIAMS

*Boundless: Your How-To Guide to Practical Remote Viewing —
Phase One is the first in a series of easy-learning manuals; each
one designed to take you through an exciting odyssey into the far
reaches of time and space via the best of all vehicles: the
subconscious mind. Join author Lori Williams as she shares her
own journey from missionary and social worker to professional
Remote Viewer, and discover how easily you, too, can use your
innate abilities to improve your relationships, your career, and
your life.*

PHASE ONE

Join Lori Lambert Williams
for a FREE 4-part Introduction to
Practical Remote Viewing Masterclass here:

https://IntuitiveSpecialists.com/masterclass-series/book/

ISBN: 978-0-9994289-2-4

Printed in the United States of America

Boundless: Your How-To Guide to Practical Remote Viewing - Phase One
by Lori Lambert Williams
Cover Design by Michelle Ivanovich
Illustrations by Lori Lambert Williams

First Edition, 2019

To Jim

All those gorgeous stars we see every night

Don't compare to you.

With all my love.

CONTENTS

My mentors, Lyn Buchanan (far left), Mel Riley (center) and me. Here, we were together at the first-ever conference of the newly-formed International Remote Viewing Association in 1999, held at the Inn of the Mountain Gods in Ruidoso, New Mexico.

A WORD FROM LYN BUCHANAN

Lyn was in the Stargate Unit, the military psychic
spying program, and like the other viewers, had several
duties. He managed the database, which allowed him to see
what worked and what didn't work in the techniques that
were being tested and developed. He also taught Controlled
Remote Viewing—a skill that he took with him when he
retired and began teaching civilians how to remote view.

I was one of the Controlled Remote Viewers for the U.S. military—an intelligence gathering process that the press later glorified with the term, "Psychic Spies". We used a protocol developed for Stanford Research Institute International by a man named Ingo Swann.

The military unit, in its various covert instances, had been under the auspices of the National Security Agency (NSA), the Central Intelligence Agency (CIA), and the Defense Intelligence Agency (DIA). When I was assigned to the unit, it had already been in existence for about ten years. It was very small as military units go, consisting of only six viewers, one director, and one secretary.

I had been assigned to the unit in 1984 because I was involved in an unusual incident in Germany, parts of which are still classified. The Controlled Remote Viewing unit was located at that time at Ft. Meade, Maryland. Because of the small number of personnel, we all "wore many hats" (meaning we had to do the various jobs of a full-sized unit).

I took over the positions of viewer, database manager, property book holder, training officer and various other jobs that had

3

previously been held by an outgoing member, Joseph McMoneagle.

The skill we used is called 'Controlled Remote Viewing' (CRV)—a misnomer, for sure, because the "viewing" part incorporates all the senses, not just the visual one. Surprisingly, the technology of CRV itself was never classified. But the fact that the military was using it, the existence of our unit and the work we were doing with it was classified. Our work was given the added distinction of "SAP", meaning, "Special Access Project". That is, even someone with a top-secret clearance did not automatically have the right or ability to know about us or our work. Even knowledge of the existence of the military unit, itself, was by "special access" only.

Within two years—working eight hours a day, five days a week—I had become fully trained and experienced in the skill of CRV and became the unit's trainer. Almost eight and a half years later, I retired from the service, but continued training CRV to a few people in the government who had the special access required to know about us, and wanted to also be trained, personally.

In late 1995, the CIA decided to declassify the project, and it became public knowledge, and public demand for the training became rampant.

I think it was back in the Dark Ages of 1996 (November of 1996, to be exact) when I had only been training CRV to the public for a little over a year, that I got a call from Lori Lambert (now, Lori Williams) asking if she could discuss the subject of remote viewing with me. She came by the house and we spent an entire evening in that discussion.

Unlike most of the other people interested in CRV at the time, Lori showed a great deal of knowledge and experience, and I agreed to train her in the technology of CRV. She progressed very quickly in her ability to do the work. In fact, she became quite accomplished at it.

Somewhere around 2001, she asked whether or not she was qualified to teach it. My first thought was, "No!" I'm very protective of the CRV method and at that time I thought that she had not had the "in the trenches" experience that we had had in the military and that I had had working for police departments and other agencies.

But then I decided that, yes, she did have the skills and a complete knowledge of the technique, so why not give it a try. She had been attending all my classes, driving back and forth from Texas to New Mexico nearly every other weekend since 1999, when she completed Advanced CRV.

Lori taught a few classes, and I waited to see how the abilities of her students would turn out. I have always known that the only judge of a good teacher is to see what his/her students can do. Her students wound up doing very well, indeed, and producing high quality work.

Even then, I had still only certified her to teach the basic level classes. Some years later, she asked whether or not I thought that she was qualified to teach the higher levels of CRV. My first thought was again, "No! You're not trained and experienced enough!" But I decided that it was time to see whether or not she was ready to do so. She and her husband, Jim, traveled with me to Dublin Ireland, and we co-taught classes there. I saw that she was clearly ready.

About that same time, she wanted to form her own CRV training company, so I told her that, since I knew that my manuals were accurate for training CRV, she could just change the logo from my company to hers, and that way, she would have the training material already in place for her company. I have not regretted that decision since.

Lori and I have both continued to train all levels in the U.S. and other countries, and now, other students who have become qualified and certified to train are beginning to train at the higher levels, as well. I have received many of her students for continuing courses, and many of my students have continued with her.

The end result is that there are now many CRV-trained students working for detective agencies and other lines of work in the civilian arena on a semi-professional and professional basis. And that is a major point in what Lori, the other qualified trainers, and I do.

From day one of the basic course, we train the students towards working at a professional level. Whether they ever make it their profession or not, if they are serious and steadfast in their training, they become capable of doing the remote viewing work at a level needed by corporations, agencies, and even governments. They are often called on (and paid) to work real-world projects as teams. They learn to do the work properly for their own lives and for the benefit of their family and friends, without any "woo-woo" factor.

What Lori teaches is a scientifically developed and proven methodology that trains a person to use his/her intuitive ability to gain information about the real world. There is no "you-will-meet-a-tall-dark-handsome-stranger" factor to what she teaches.

The CRV method is geared towards helping humanity, bringing home missing children, finding missing evidence for police departments, working medical cases, technological R&D projects, helping with corporate planning, and even helping themselves prosper.

We have worked projects for moon exploration companies, police departments in various countries, locating mineral and oil deposits for mining companies, stock market investing, and even such lowly, but real-world goals as going to casinos and coming back out with more money in our pockets than when we went in.

I am very happy to see that Lori has written this book. I believe that it will help bring a new, higher level of mental abilities and purposes to humanity, and that, as the saying goes, "this rising tide will wind up lifting all ships".

What Lori is teaching and writing about in this and other of her books will help any reader who is serious about doing the work to elevate his/her life, thoughts, prosperity, and goals, and in the process, lift the level of human awareness.

If you are in possession of this book, you have in your hands a training manual for a better life and future. Do the work. Practice diligently. The end result will be amazing to you.

Lyn Buchanan
Former military remote viewer with the Stargate Unit,
Fort Meade, Maryland

A WORD FROM MEL RILEY

Mel Riley was the first official Remote Viewer for the U.S. government's Psychic Spy Program, Ft. Meade, Maryland, and the only Remote Viewer in the military's 20-year program to serve two tours of duty in the unit.

I've known Lori Williams for over 20 years. We met at the first-ever International Remote Viewing Association (IRVA) conference in Ruidoso, New Mexico on the White Mountain Apache reservation. I was signing in to the conference when my old friend, Lyn Buchanan, walked up.

"I've got somebody you have to meet!" he said enthusiastically. "She is a rising star, one of my best pupils." That is how I remember meeting Lori. That was back in 1999.

Since that first meeting, Lori and I have worked on several Controlled Remote Viewing (CRV) projects together and I have sat in on several of her classes. I have no hesitation to recommend her training programs, either in person, on-line or through this book.

As far as I'm concerned, Lori is one of the best CRV trainers you can have as you learn this incredible skill. First of all, she was trained by the best. Lori is the protégé of my colleague, Lyn Buchanan. Lyn and I were among the original members of the U.S. military's "psychic spying" unit in Ft. Meade, Maryland, where CRV was used in real-world tasking on foreign military and political targets.

Lori became Lyn's protégé and he trained her with the same rigor and discipline with which he trained the military's viewers. She took the best of what Lyn taught her and made it her own.

Her teaching style is very approachable, she has a great sense of humor and her students excel. Lori has a solid foundation in the structure and protocols developed by the military, yet she makes CRV fun and easy to learn.

Not only is she a wonderful instructor, but Lori also practices what she teaches. She is a well-respected professional viewer. I have recommended Lori many times to people looking for a seasoned professional for operational targets (targets for which viewers are hired).

It's important for operational viewers to be objective, keep their cool and not be overwhelmed by what they find. Lori is unflappable as a viewer. She's a real pro!

We once worked on a pretty wild target together. It was a double-blind target—which means that neither of us knew the nature of the target. The only information we had was the target coordinates.

I was the first one to do the session and evidently, the requester was impressed with what I found. The requester asked me if I knew anybody else that I thought was mature enough to work on the project. I still didn't know what I had viewed, but I suggested Lori.

When I found out what the project was—I have to admit that I was concerned for Lori. This was many years ago. Back then, I didn't know if she had ever done an esoteric target (a target with little or no verifiable feedback) or if she was ready for the subject matter of this particular "out there" target. I was also concerned that she might object to this project because of the nature of the target.

But she did two full sessions on this target, and whether it affected her or not—and regardless of what she may or may not have thought about the nature of the target—she worked her way

10

through the session like a pro and had some *very* interesting results.

To this day I don't know that there's any provable feedback from that target (because no one has been to Mars yet) but it was interesting when we compared what we found during our sessions.

We discovered that our findings were pretty similar which gave us both the feeling that we were on target, wherever it was. And our subsequent communications about our findings and the deeply profound impact the sessions had on us both cemented an already-close friendship.

Before I end this endorsement of Lori and her work, I just want you to know that there are some people out there trying to teach remote viewing who don't have a clue. Some are just trying to make money. They've read someone else's manual and then they teach CRV without ever having done a professional target.

But I can guarantee you that Lori can teach CRV and she can do it, too! She *is* a professional remote viewer.

Whatever your reason for wanting to learn CRV, if you learn the proper methodology and practice, remote viewing can improve your life.

And there is no one better to start you on this journey than Lori Williams. I encourage you to read *Boundless: Your How-To Guide to Practical Remote Viewing* and practice the exercises.

This will get you started, and her subsequent remote viewing 'how to' books will be equally good, I'm sure. Lori really cares about her students—and that means you—and she is putting terrific detail into these books. Best of all, Lori makes learning to remote view really *FUN!*

BOUNDLESS: PHASE ONE

Melvin Riley
The first official Remote Viewer
for the U.S. government's Psychic Spy Program,
Ft. Meade, Maryland

THIS BOOK IS FOR YOU IF . . .

This book is for you if—

- you have been seeking for a way to increase *and control* your own intuitive abilities.

- you are ready to put in the work required to develop your skills.

- you are excited to explore the depths of Consciousness itself.

- you have an open mind and are excited to learn new things.

- you have the drive, determination, and discipline to work through the various levels of progress until you achieve mastery.

This book is NOT for you if—

- you have a mental illness that would make this course contraindicated for you.

- you are frustrated easily.

- you give up easily.

- you have no patience.

- you think that your intuitive sense is somehow evil (any more than your other five senses would be).

- you hate structure.

- you would prefer not to have to work to achieve a goal worth attaining.

Know that learning Controlled Remote Viewing (CRV) will require the utmost in patience.

And you will learn a LOT about yourself along the way.

Lastly, understand that the word 'control' in Controlled Remote Viewing is all about *controlling yourself.* No one else will control you. You are in charge at all times. In order to gain mastery of your own intuitive abilities, you need to learn to control them.

The goal in learning Controlled Remote Viewing is to reach a point where *you* determine when, where, and how your abilities manifest.

My name is Lori Williams, and I'll be your instructor on this amazing journey you are about to undertake. I have been teaching CRV since 2001. My goal as your instructor is to ensure that I present this information to you in an easy-to-learn, step-by-step format. In addition to this book, look for *Boundless* Books two through six. These books will also be offered as interactive e-books with accompanying video instruction. For those who find they need something more personal or visual, my full online courses will soon be available on video.

If you would like to take the full Basic CRV course, you can take a live 3-day workshop with me by checking out the calendar on our website at https://intuitivespecialists.com/events/

If you are interested in learning more or just checking out what a video course might be like, here is a link to a FREE 4-part introduction to Practical Remote Viewing, or PRV. To access the free course, sign up here:

https://intuitivespecialists.com/masterclass-series-introduction/

We also offer a fun 6-week video course that you can take at your leisure. If you are interested in taking the full 6-week course, you can read all about it here:

https://intuitivespecialists.com/practical-remote-viewing/

This is the same information contained in my live CRV Basic course, but just in a format that allows you to study the full course on your own schedule, as your time permits.

Once you have taken either the 3-day Basic CRV workshop or the 6-week Video PRV course, you will receive a free one-month membership in the amazing online Club CRV!

In the club, you will receive weekly content from me, and will have access to recorded trainings, a private community located within our own Kajabi platform (no Facebook!), CRV session demonstrations, bonus materials, mentoring meetings, and once-a-month live Q&A sessions.

Why the Club? You take the course to learn the structure. You join the club to gain *Mastery*. Being part of a vital community of like-minded folks *inspires* you to *practice*, and it keeps you motivated, learning, and excited about your new skill!

MODULE I:

The Basics

INTRODUCTION

IMAGINE . . .

If you had a magic carpet that could take you anywhere in all of Time and Space, where would you go? What would you want to see first? Would you travel back in Time to visit your great-great-grandfather? Would you witness the building of the pyramids? Would you fly forward to see what the planet looks like two hundred years from now? Perhaps you would want to visit other galaxies or find out what it feels like to be microscopic.

Good news: You ***do*** have that magic carpet! And it is built in! What is it called, you ask? That one is easy to answer: *Consciousness.*

Many of us simply want to figure out how to have better relationships or more abundance. And most of us just want to be happy or find the right career or run our businesses more efficiently. What about pollution or global warming? What should we do about that?

What do *you* want most? And what do you need to find it?

Again, thankfully, you have all the answers right inside of you: *Consciousness!*

Consciousness seems to be quite the buzzword nowadays, and many people are using it. But the truth is it is a pretty exciting word! Quantum physics is beginning to prove that consciousness is much more than we ever realized, and it has the ability to allow humans to travel backwards and forwards through Time, as well as exploring the far reaches of Space.

"Ok," you think, "but how can **I** access that magic carpet?"

19

This is where Controlled Remote Viewing comes in. Controlled Remote Viewing can allow you to do and have all of the above—and *much* more.

You may have heard the term 'Remote Viewing' and thought that it represented what Madam Minerva does in her gypsy tent. But it was actually developed as a top-secret 'psychic spying program' by Stanford Research Institute for the U.S. Military. (More about that later.)

Once the top-secret program was declassified, many of the military men who had taught remote viewing in the Stargate Unit received phone calls from people with comments like "I have been a Remote Viewer all my life! I am a *crystal ball* Remote Viewer!"

Others would say they remote viewed using runes, or psychometry, or palm reading. All of these techniques are interesting and have merit when used in the correct manner, but they are not truly 'Controlled Remote Viewing'.

Perhaps you've even picked up some terrific books about Controlled Remote Viewing and the history of the military's top-secret program. But the one thing difficult to find in any of those books is a set of very down-to-earth instructions showing you *how to do it*, written clearly in a way that is easy to understand and follow. If you are looking for the nuts and bolts of the structure, the format and the real ins and outs of Remote Viewing—you have come to the right place!

This book covers the first phase of the Controlled Remote Viewing process. I tell my students, "If you can learn this first part, everything else from here will seem easy!"

That's right: This book will shatter some of your paradigms, your preconceived notions, and it may introduce ideas you've never thought of before. And because it's new, like anything new you've chosen to learn, this part may seem harder than anything that comes after. Take your time. Be patient with yourself. Enjoy the process. And above all—just jump in with an open mind.

I am writing this Phase 1 book as though everyone who reads it will continue on to become proficient in the subsequent phases. This first book in the series will give you the background and foundation you need to proceed to *Boundless: Phase 2*.

My husband, CRV monitor and life partner is Jim Williams. Jim and I will be doing live demonstrations of the process periodically on Zoom webinars. And all our video demonstrations will be available in the archive for those who join our Club CRV! By watching videoed demonstrations, you'll be able to see and learn from visual examples. And if you have any questions about the process, you can jump on our exclusive CRV community forum to get answers from me or a member of my team.

You can watch the videos at your convenience, stop the recording whenever you want or need to, and replay any parts for which you need clarification—and best of all, you will have access to the videos for life. I will be available once a week to answer questions in the forum.

Where will this journey take you? Keep reading to find out!

YOUR ROAD MAP

Before we go any further, I'd like to give you a bird's eye view of what's ahead. Many people just don't know what to expect.

"Will I be using a crystal ball? Will I go into a trance?" they wonder.

The answer is no.

Controlled Remote Viewing is a process wherein a Remote Viewer (that's you) will sit at a table with some blank white printer paper and a black gel pen. With your eyes open, wide awake, you will follow a written, structured protocol to put your thoughts on paper.

The written structure of CRV helps to separate ordinary imagination and random thoughts from true psychic perceptions.

CRV is composed of six phases, each of which has its own function and set of guidelines. The book you are holding in your hand (or on your device) is the first of a set of six. Each book covers a different phase of the CRV structure.

This first book, *Boundless: Phase One,* is special. Why? First, because it covers Phase 1 of the Controlled Remote Viewing process. Phase 1 is the most important phase of all because it creates the foundation for all the other phases. But this first book also gives you a wealth of background information that you will need to gain a full understanding of the Controlled Remote Viewing process.

Note: Just to give you a heads up, as I continue to add to the *Boundless* series, upcoming books will use the term *Practical Remote Viewing* and *PRV* instead of *Controlled Remote Viewing* and *CRV*. We want to emphasize the importance of learning this amazing skill as a very *practical* tool in your day-to-day life.

CHAPTER ONE:

WHAT *IS* 'CONTROLLED REMOTE VIEWING'?

We all experience sporadic bursts of intuition. Everyone knows how it feels to just 'know in your gut'. Have you ever felt that you should do a certain thing, and when you did it, you found out it was perfect timing or that you avoided disaster? Or have you ever *not* done something you just *knew* you should do? Yeah . . . me, too! I know how awful that feels.

For most of us, that is the extent of our intuitive experiences. That is 'normal'. There are those who experience more than that. These rare individuals have precognitive dreams—dreams that foretell the future in some way—or they have visions about something occurring in a far distant land, or they see ghosts, or have other paranormal experiences.

We tend to fear that which we do not understand, so it can be scary to have experiences such as those mentioned above. It is especially frightening when these experiences are not controlled. They happen unexpectedly, whenever or wherever they want to. This is what I refer to as 'the tail wagging the dog'.

But what if you *could* control these experiences? We all have intuitive abilities that are inherent in our human being-ness. The problem is that we don't know how to access these abilities on demand or how to separate true intuitive perceptions from mere imagination.

The human mind is a fascinating place. It has many facets, and they are all just waiting to be explored. We know our minds have great capacity and that we only use a tiny portion of that capacity. Controlled Remote Viewing, or CRV, allows you to use *more* of your mind.

I like to think of CRV as a drawer organizer for the brain. We all have a junk drawer. You know what I mean: that drawer full of rubber bands, paper clips, toothpicks, screws, half-used Super Glue tubes, and things we'd rather not imagine. The messiness of it bugs you, so you run to Walmart (or wherever you run) and you find a drawer organizer! This gadget has cubbyholes for everything! Now you have a place for those rubber bands and paper clips! Each item has an assigned compartment in the drawer, and things are nice and neat from now on.

Our thoughts often feel frantic or scrambled just like that junk drawer. We may suffer from information overload. This world in which we live is so busy, and we now have access to news 24/7 via social media, the Internet and TV. It can feel pretty tricky, trying to figure out which random thoughts contain valid intuitive information and which thoughts are just nonsense, opinions, or imagination.

CRV can help you sort through the mess and develop a great working relationship with your own subconscious mind. The key to what makes CRV so versatile (and therefore superior, in my opinion, to other methods of remote viewing) lies in the word *control*. This is *Controlled* Remote Viewing.

Think of any martial art. What does it take to go from being a white belt (novice) to becoming a tenth-degree black belt? (Hint: How do you get to Carnegie Hall?) That's right: Practice, practice, practice! And CRV is very much a martial art. You will learn foundational steps and then build on those steps until they become second nature.

When you learn a martial art, you practice the steps over and over until you know them so well, they become automatic. If someone attacks you, you respond without thinking, because you are so well trained. This is the way CRV works. You will learn the written structure, which seems complex at first. Once the structure is a part of you and you can work through it without thinking, you will build on that, adding more layers and more techniques.

Eventually, you'll find that CRV is like a fancy Swiss Army knife with all sorts of bells and whistles—extremely versatile. And with diligent practice, your own abilities to solve problems, obtain needed information, and find a multitude of details about something will be practically limitless!

Now I know you are anxious to get to those nuts and bolts I promised you—and we will. It is very important for me to give you a firm foundation of understanding on which to build. As soon as I've done that, we are going to jump into the 'how-to' part of this amazing skill.

Throughout this book, I will be providing illustrations, stories, and analogies that will make the Controlled Remote Viewing process much easier to understand. As someone who has dedicated her life since 1996 to the study of this fascinating science, rest assured that *you* are what I care about most.

Your safety, your understanding, and your achieving competence in using your mind to access information throughout Time and Space are my priorities in bringing this information to you in book form. What you are about to read is the *exact* information I have been teaching to my students—many of whom are now professional Remote Viewers—all over the world, since 2001.

CHAPTER TWO:

WHAT YOU CAN EXPECT FROM THIS BOOK

This book covers the foundation of CRV, including the background information, preparation for your session, the administrative section, and most importantly, Ideograms—the written, symbolic language that can open the door between your conscious and subconscious minds, allowing intuitive information to flow.

I will thoroughly cover the first phase of Controlled Remote Viewing. We refer to this phase as 'Phase 1' or 'P1'. (You may occasionally hear people refer to the phases as *stages*. You can call them either one and still be correct. In my classes, I refer to them as Phases.)

Boundless: Phase One is the first in a series of six books. The information in this series is presented sequentially so that you can focus on mastering the information you gain from one book before moving on to the next, without getting too overwhelmed.

These books are designed to be *very* comprehensive and complete. I love being able to put this into print, because we aren't limited by three-day workshops! You get to have it ALL—right here in these pages. And what you do with this knowledge is up to you.

You may find that the information in this first book is a bit more difficult to grasp than your average course in metaphysics. Phase 1 of the CRV process is very different from anything you have learned to date. For that reason, you might find it more challenging than anything you will ever learn in any remote viewing course you ever take!

You will be literally learning a new language, and that is never easy. The information will create a new paradigm for you. As a result, it might feel a bit tough in the beginning. But if you work through that and hang in there with me, it gets easier from there—I promise!

Boundless Books One through Three cover what I teach in my Basic Controlled Remote Viewing Foundational Course. For those who want more: If you really apply yourself and learn these techniques, you may choose to go on to the Intermediate Level, which you will find in Books Four and Five. And if you are really wild, after Intermediate CRV, you have the option to go on to the Advanced Level in Book Six!

Learning something from a book can be particularly challenging. My son-in-law taught himself guitar from books, and he is now truly a professional guitarist! But I don't know many people who have that kind of discipline. I know that I don't! I needed a guide, an instructor.

To address that issue, we offer various forms of follow up to fit every personality. If you just want to dabble, you may decide to read the book, do a little practice and that is it.

For those who are truly serious about becoming world-class-level Remote Viewers, this book is just the beginning. The student who is focused and has the motivation to go all the way will want to sign up for in-person or online live courses and ride this train as far as it will go!

Those who aspire to become professional Remote Viewers go on to study with me in my mentoring clubs, building their skills continually through daily, weekly, and monthly assignments until they become fully competent. Some students have gone on to become 'Operational Remote Viewers', working on real-world projects, helping to find missing people, discovering buried treasure, seeking solutions to problems for themselves and others.

As we study the many parts of this mental martial art, I've organized the information into modules, which are then broken down into chapters.

There are exercises within the book designed to enhance your observational skills, improve your ability to describe and increase your vocabulary. You'll also find opportunities to practice what you have learned.

By the end of the Basic Course (Books One to Three)—if you take your time and practice faithfully—you will be able to describe a target far removed from you in Time and Space. You will be able to write a summary of your findings, including the sensory (such as colors, textures, temperatures, tastes, sounds, smells) and dimensional (shapes, sizes, patterns, positions, measures, and so on) aspects of a target, and you will be able to sketch aspects of the target. You will learn to categorize and score your sessions for accuracy and how to gain the most from each session through a process called Post Session Analysis.

After you have learned the basics of CRV, I will teach you what to do when you want to remote view something that is very near and dear to your heart—something so personal to you that you cannot think of it without emotion. Those are the hardest targets to view.

You will be prepared to view a variety of targets, including manmade objects, people, events, activities and locations, and you will gain an understanding of how your newly acquired talents can be used in a plethora of practical day-to-day applications.

All of this ties together to assist you in improving your decisions, your choices, and your life.

What Is a 'Target'?

A target can be just about anything. Whatever a remote viewer chooses or is asked to remote view is known as 'the target'. It can be an object, a location, an activity, an event, a person, an animal, a journey, a technology, an archeological site, or anything else. So, whenever I refer to a 'target' in this manual, know that I mean whatever the viewer is viewing.

A 'hard target' means a target that is provable, knowable, and something for which there is or will be solid, demonstrable feedback. If you are the Viewer, and after your session I pull out a photograph of what you have been viewing so that you can score your session summary, that means you just viewed a 'hard target'. The photograph is known as 'feedback'.

An 'esoteric target' is one for which there may never be any feedback. *"What do the extraterrestrials on the planet Xerxes in the galaxy Zebulon look like?"* would be an example of an esoteric target. We don't bother with those—for now, at least. Once a Viewer has become a very advanced Remote Viewer and has a provable track record showing his or her degree of accuracy on hard targets, then we can trust that person's results on unprovable targets.

The ultimate goal is to learn a skill that is dependable, accurate and useful in practical ways to help you navigate through life's many challenges and events with joy and confidence.

CHAPTER THREE:

PRACTICAL USES OF CRV

Why *do* people sign up to learn CRV, anyway? One of the questions I am asked most frequently is "What are some ways that this technique is used nowadays?"

CRV can be used to—

- Improve strategic planning for corporations and companies.

- Assist law enforcement to find missing people and provide information that can help them to solve crimes.

- Locate artifacts and structures in important archeological searches.

- Help parents better understand their children and foresee problems before they occur.

- Work with medical personnel to detect illness and locate the source.

- Improve creativity for authors, songwriters and more.

- Uncover hidden secrets of history.

- Describe future technologies.

- Devise improved strategies and processes for current methods of doing things.

- Find solutions to personal, professional, and planetary issues.

- Make better life choices.

A COUPLE OF EXAMPLES

Fear of Heights

Prior to becoming involved in CRV, I had a terrible fear of heights. Being up in a building, roller coasters, tree houses—the thought of anything high up—caused my heart to pound and my breathing to seize up.

I didn't make a big deal out of my phobia, but when I started working with my mentor Lyn Buchanan, he noticed that whenever he would give me a remote viewing target that involved heights, I would have a visible reaction. After several episodes of me being unable to view these high targets, he finally asked, "Are you afraid of heights?" I responded with an emphatic "YES."

After that, Lyn made a point to send me targets with heights involved. I viewed airplanes in flight, hot air balloons, Cirque de Soleil acrobats in the air, the highest roller coaster in the world, and many other targets involving heights. He would mix these targets into a packet of non-height-related targets. After several months, I became desensitized to heights.

The real test came when I went to visit my son, who was stationed at Cape Canaveral in Florida. It was shortly after the tragic events of 9/11, and Busch Gardens Amusement Park opened its doors to active military and their families. Busch Gardens is known for its HUGE roller coasters.

The park was almost deserted, so we didn't have to wait in lines to ride anything—so ride we did! Sailing along atop high roller coasters all day long, I was the only one who didn't get sick! It was a good test of my newfound cure for phobias: CRV!

Since then, I have gone parasailing 600 feet above the ocean attached to a kite; I've been dropped 300 feet while wrapped like a burrito hooked to a bungee cord; and have been on many death-defying extremely high amusement park rides—all done with a great amount of joy and very little fear.

Helping an Archeologist

Although I am limited in what I am allowed to share publicly about this next example, I do have permission to share some of the fascinating details.

A while back, we had a wonderful opportunity to mount a major remote viewing project with an archeologist who had been looking for artifacts in a 200-square mile section of ocean—for forty years! Enlisting the skills of twelve Remote Viewers and four Project Managers, the project began.

The only information the viewers were given was: "The target is a location. Describe the target."

All the viewers began by viewing something tall, tower-like and metallic. As the target was in the ocean, we called the archeologist to ask about this.

"Oh, yes! A mile away from the site is a floating naval communications tower," he responded.

Great! A confirmation that the viewers were on target.

After the viewers had established what we refer to as good 'site contact' (meaning we knew they were on the right target), we sent them all a blank map with only the corners marked. The viewers viewed the most important places on that map and marked them.

Once we had received the maps back from the viewers, we were able to create transparencies of each map. Then, by placing the transparencies on top of each other, we could see the areas of agreement.

Writing up an extensive report for the archeologist, complete with GPS coordinates, we were excited to send in the results of the first completed segment of the project.

The archeologist took boats, divers, and equipment to one of the GPS coordinates and found the artifacts for which he had been searching forty years! These artifacts—engraved walls, archways, and pillars—were located in an area that has been covered with ocean for 18,000 years. A very exciting find!

Does this mean that a civilization once existed at this location before it became inundated with ocean? And if so, were there civilizations on earth more than 18,000 years ago?

This is just one example of what operational Controlled Remote Viewing can do. Professional Remote Viewers and experienced Project Managers make an unbeatable team.

At this point, someone always asks me, "Can anyone do this?" Read on to find out.

CHAPTER FOUR:

CAN ANYONE DO IT?

The answer is a resounding YES! I've never had a student who couldn't do it. That inevitably prompts the silent question, *"What if I am the first one?"* No worries! Keep reading.

I once had a student who was in his mid-seventies. He had difficulty remembering the structure. The other students in the class were quickly blowing past him in their structural accuracy and their results. I worried about him, but I needn't have.

A few months later, this man called me and wanted to register for my Intermediate course. Thinking to myself that he had barely passed the Basic course, I tried to dissuade him. Thankfully, he was a stubborn ol' coot, and he refused to take 'no' for an answer.

Imagine my surprise when he showed up to my Intermediate class and began doing a demo for me. His structure was perfect! And he nailed the target! I couldn't hide my amazement as I asked him how he had gone from zero to one hundred in a few short months.

"Practice." he replied. "Since your Basic course a few months ago, I have read the manual several times and I have done over 300 practice sessions."

"No wonder!" I thought. The moral of this story is that *anyone* can do this!

At the time of this writing, I have taught CRV to nearly a thousand students ranging in age from twelve to eighty-seven years old. While age may play a role in how quickly one grasps information and in how long one retains it, I have not found it to be a major impediment to learning.

Over the years, I have had the occasional student grappling with short-term memory issues due to, for example, a closed head injury. For that reason, I created a series of templates, cue cards and even a cheat sheet to help my students remember the structure and other details of the Controlled Remote Viewing process. I will be here to hold your hand and teach you all the insider secrets that will make your journey smoother.

CHAPTER FIVE:

MY STORY

Like all of us, my story is a rather unusual one, and as I tell you a bit about myself, please don't feel that *your* story has to be like *my* story.

Everyone's story is unique. You are special, and as we work together, you will be building on to the stories you've experienced thus far in your life. You don't need to have had any prior 'mystical events', near-death experiences, or to have seen angels or spirits. Just the fact that you are *human* is all you need to learn CRV.

August of 1991 found my family and me back in the Continental USA after many years abroad doing missionary work. I felt like an alien from a foreign planet. So many things had changed! My children had never seen a gumball machine, or a pop-top can. The tried-and-true phone company I had always known, 'Ma Bell', was judged to be a monopoly. As a result, I was unable to make a long-distance phone call from a pay phone because I didn't know what a 'long distance carrier' was. I had never heard of a W-2 form or an insurance deductible because I had never filed taxes or had any form of insurance.

Even with those odds, I called a wrong number a few days after arriving, and secured a decent job as a social worker, working for the State of Texas Department of Human Services in Amarillo, Texas. Five years later, in 1996, I was hired by a local non-profit agency to become their Director of Resettlement in a program that resettled refugees.

Around that time, I had decided that I needed to reconcile the many paranormal experiences I had had all my life with the belief system I had held for the past twenty years. Since I had been attempting—and failing—to avoid any contact or discussion of the supernatural, my decision to revisit those experiences was a bold one at the time. It felt as though I was treading dangerous ground, perhaps even getting in league with the devil! (Don't laugh.)

So, I needed to tread carefully, I thought. I didn't want to jump into bed with the first warlock I could find! Instead, I was searching for true answers to our nature as human beings. When I became a Christian missionary, I thought I could leave my precognitive dreams, my seeing of spirits and my psychic 'knowing' behind me. Instead, all of my abilities seemed to increase in strength and occurrence.

"How could this be evil?" I wondered. I had dedicated twenty years of my life to God, and yet, I was still receiving spontaneous psychic information, having precognitive dreams, and seeing spirits on occasion.

"I know I am not evil!" I thought. "Therefore, there *must* be a reasonable explanation—one that *doesn't* involve demon possession!"

Shortly after I was hired at the non-profit, I was sent to Denver, Colorado, to attend a conference at the Spring Institute regarding Secondary Post-Traumatic Stress Disorder. The speakers were fantastic. Among them was a recently retired colonel who shared his expertise as a psychologist about the various aspects of PTSD.

I was fascinated by the topic. That night, I dreamed of the colonel. Only a few days earlier in Amarillo, I had met another retired colonel, the first colonel I had ever met. In my dream, I was asking the psychologist-colonel if he knew the retired colonel I had just met in Amarillo. Then I woke up.

The next morning, arriving early for the conference, I found myself alone with the psychologist-colonel outside the ballroom doors. In one of those embarrassing moments, I blurted out to this total stranger, "I had a dream about you last night!"

Now, my mother used to jokingly tell me, "If you want a man to remember you, just tell him you had a dream about him." That, however, was not my intention at the time, I promise!

Looking somewhat surprised, the colonel asked, "Really? Tell me about your dream."

I proceeded to tell him about the dream, which prompted him to ask, "In what branch of the military is this colonel that you met?"

"I'm not sure," I replied, "I think he was in military intelligence."

"Funny," said the colonel, "*I* was in military intelligence."

At that moment, the cover of a book I had just seen on the New Arrivals shelf flashed in front of my mind's eye. Again, without thinking, I blurted, "Have you seen that new book?!!" (Inwardly, I was thinking, "Ugh. Did I just say that with my Out Loud Voice?")

"What book?" asked the colonel.

"I can't remember the name of it. It is turquoise and black on the cover, and it has something to do with psychics in the military," I quickly replied.

"Are you talking about *Psychic Warrior* by David Morehouse?" he almost shouted.

"Yes! Yes! That's it!" I exclaimed.

"I cannot believe you are asking me about that book," he responded with amazement. "I was the psychologist in charge of that program for twenty years."

He leaned in, peering into my eyes with newfound interest.

41

"Do you remember maps easily? Do you have a photographic memory for numbers? Are you artistic?" The questions flowed.

"Yes," I replied, as visions of men in black suits carrying me away in unmarked cars floated through my mind.

As I slowly began backing away from him, the colonel called to me: "When you get home, look up Controlled Remote Viewing!"

You can imagine that the first thing I did when I got home was to look up Controlled Remote Viewing.

The Internet, at least for the general public, was still in its infancy in 1996, but a website quickly appeared. The words "What is CRV?" were big and bold on the screen in front of my eyes. I drank in every word with a sense of recognition, as though I was coming home.

The website belonged to a retired military man and former Methodist minister named Lyn Buchanan. Lyn had been one of the Remote Viewers in the military's top-secret psychic spying unit, known most commonly as 'Stargate'. His explanation of how our intuition works sounded very intelligent and well grounded.

I liked how he mentioned intuition as simply a part of being human. Suddenly, it wasn't associated with the devil anymore in my mind. I knew I had found what I had been searching for. I sent Lyn an inquiry email, which he answered kindly and thoroughly.

As synchronicity would have it, I ended up stuck at another weekend conference in Baltimore only two short weeks later. With great fear and trepidation (because at the time, it was supposedly quite dangerous to contact people you met on the Internet) I called Lyn. He and his wife welcomed me into their home, where we talked for five hours, non-stop.

From that moment on, Lyn became my mentor, and for the next ten years he taught me with an intensity and dedication I have so come to admire in him . . . Eventually, he certified me to teach CRV.

According to Lyn's handwritten dedication in my copy of his book, *The Seventh Sense*, I had become "the first civilian certified to teach Controlled Remote Viewing".

It was in 2001 that Lyn began turning over some Basic courses to me to teach for him. In early 2002, I was going through a divorce and the non-profit I worked for was reeling from the events of 9/11. My boss wasn't sure the agency would survive. By turning over a huge piece of his business to me, Lyn wanted to be sure I would be able to take care of myself and my children as a single mom. That was such a generous act of kindness; to this day, I am still overwhelmed when I think of it.

During this time, I continued to be mentored by Lyn and assisted him in class as he taught the Intermediate and Advanced level courses, while handling many of his U.S.-based Basic courses. In 2007, Lyn and I traveled to Ireland to teach in Dublin.

Finally, in early 2010, after nine years of training with him and teaching for his company, Lyn and his lovely wife, Linda, let me know that it was time for me to fly alone. After giving me a year to prepare, they gently pushed me out of the nest on January 1, 2011 to teach on my own, no longer under the comforting umbrella of their company. I was flying solo for the first time, teaching all levels of Controlled Remote Viewing, Associative Remote Viewing, and Extended Remote Viewing under the auspices of my own company.

Although it was scary—and a LOT more work to handle all the details of running my own business—pushing me out of the nest was the greatest gift they could have given me. I gained confidence and now had more control over every aspect of my company.

Along the way, I became friends with another legendary military Remote Viewer, Melvin Riley. Mel has the distinction of being the first soldier inducted into the newly-created Military Remote Viewing Unit, and the only person who served two tours within that unit. Mel also became my friend, mentor and confidant.

A gifted natural psychic in his own right, Mel's perspective on CRV and remote viewing in general amplified my understanding and gave me a more robust understanding of intuition in general.

When something *really* weird happens—the sort of thing you just don't want to tell anyone for fear they may think you insane—Mel is someone I can always turn to. His stories are phenomenal and belong in a book of their own. He, too, has been extremely generous with his time, always willing to drop whatever he is doing to speak to me when I call.

In the years since, I have become a prolific instructor of Controlled Remote Viewing, currently teaching more students more often than any other instructor, as well as being the only instructor to offer follow up instruction via online mentoring clubs.

Now that you know my story—how *I* found out about CRV—you know who it is that is teaching you. Are you ready for your own journey to begin?

Let's get started!

CHAPTER SIX:

THE LAMP ANALOGY

THE
LAMP

IS
THE "TASKER"

Think about a lamp.
The lamp needs power, right?
But we have no control over
the lamp's need for power.

The lamp in this analogy
represents the person who
needs information.

We call the person who needs
information 'The Tasker'.

For example, the detective who
needs to know the location of the
criminal is known as 'The Tasker'.

We have no control over
the Tasker's need
for information.

Think about the source of
power needed by the lamp.
The lamp needs electricity!

We will refer to
this as "The Source".

The lightning in this
image represents the
Source of Information
needed by the Tasker.

The Source may be known as
"God," or "The Akashic Records"
or even
"The Great Big Cosmic
Database in the Sky".

You are free to think of The Source
any way you choose.

The important thing to remember is:

**We do not have any control
over The Source
of the information!**

THE
ELECTRICAL
CORD

IS THE
CONDUIT,
THE CRV'er!

In order to connect the Lamp
to The Source of Power,
what do we need?

A CONDUIT.

An electric cord!

In this analogy, the conduit
is the
Controlled Remote Viewer,
or "CRV'er".

That is the <u>only</u> part
of this analogy
that can be <u>controlled</u>.

"Oh, NO!" you may be
tempted to think.
"Who will control the CRV'er???"

The answer?

YOU.

You control Yourself.

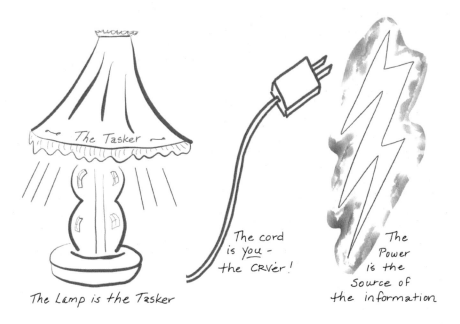

The Lamp is the Tasker

The cord is you – the CRVer!

The Power is the Source of the information

So here we have it:
The Lamp is the Tasker—the person who needs information.
The Lightning is the Source of the information.
*The electrical cord is **you**—The CRV'er.*

Controlled Remote Viewing is the controlled use of one's intuitive ability through a structured written protocol.

Controlled Remote Viewing is a tool that allows an ordinary human being to access his or her innate intuitive ability in order to obtain detailed information about anything in all of Time and/or Space.

The Controlled Remote Viewer, or CRV'er, utilizes the written structure of the CRV process to separate imagination from true psychic perceptions.

48

*The CRV protocol is a matrix, designed to assist the
Viewer to explore the various parts of the target.*

*From now on, when you want to remember the three
parts of any psychic or remote viewing process, remember
the analogy of the Lamp, the Conduit and the Source of Power:*

*In order to understand this skill to a profound degree,
it is vital to practice.
And as you practice, you will begin to understand things you
never dreamed possible! One of my students referred to CRV
as 'the ultimate self-development tool'. As a Controlled Remote
Viewer, you are going to get to know yourself very profoundly.*

Congratulations!

CHAPTER SEVEN:

A WEE BIT OF HISTORY

Many years ago, a Russian man defected to the United States. (Sorry, I was never privy to exactly *who* this man was, or what his position within the Russian military had been.)

All I know is that he carried papers with him, indicating that the Russian government had an active 'psychic spying unit'. (Ahhhh . . . So that's how they had been getting all of our best-kept secrets!)

Never to be outdone, the U.S. government decided that if the Russians had such a program, we had better find a way to develop one, too. So, with the help of two eminent scientists who had been pioneers of the laser at Stanford Research Institute, Hal Puthoff and Russell Targ, telepathy and the powers of the human mind were researched.

Hal was overseeing the program while Russ conducted most of the experiments. They gathered 'super-psychic' retired Burbank, California, police officer Pat Price and a well-known psychic artist, Ingo Swann, and began experimenting with extrasensory perception. Later, Russ' friend Hella Hammid was added to the team. In the beginning, most of the experiments involved Russ or Hal choosing a target and then Russ sitting with the Remote Viewer in a Faraday cage and asking the Viewer to relate what he or she was seeing in the mind's eye.

Because the military needed to be able to teach any soldier 'how to be psychic', Ingo was contracted to develop the structure and protocols of Controlled Remote Viewing.

At that time, this technique was known as Coordinate Remote Viewing. But eventually, the researchers discovered that coordinates were not necessary; Remote Viewers could view a target anywhere, in all of time and space, without the use of longitude and latitude!

The military used some form of remote viewing for over twenty years. This methodology was utilized to supplement intelligence information for the government. Each year, the Viewers in the unit had to do a 'dog and pony show' for the top brass in order to secure funding for the following year. The fact that they were funded year after year for twenty years is a clear indication that, contrary to later attempts to discredit the military Remote Viewers to the public, Controlled Remote Viewing was a demonstrably useful intelligence tool.

The CRV program occasionally passed from one agency to another and over the years was called by several classified code names. In 1995, the program was declassified. At that time, several of the military men who had dedicated a large part of their careers to remote viewing decided to teach it.

I am blessed to count a few of these early pioneers among my closest friends and mentors to this day, and I will be forever grateful to them for the sacred knowledge they have shared with me.

Thanks to them, I have been honored to teach CEO's of major corporations, number one New York Times best-selling authors, celebrities, film makers, law enforcement officials, medical doctors, attorneys, real estate brokers—people from all walks of life and from the four corners of the world.

My passion is to share this amazing skill with you, so that you can discover the thrill of knowing that you are so much more than your body—that you are truly BOUNDLESS.

CHAPTER EIGHT:

THE WHY'S OF
THE CRV STRUCTURE

CRV is designed to open the door between your Conscious and Subconscious Minds. It is set up in phases that allow you to move progressively from basic information to greater and greater detail.

In the beginning, think of the Conscious and Subconscious Minds as *siblings*. Remember how you used to fight with your brother or sister when you were little? Those sibling rivalries felt important at the time, as the two of you struggled to establish dominance.

The Conscious and Subconscious Minds are much like the siblings in this analogy. The Subconscious Mind runs the show, but everything it does is happening below the lid, under the covers, so to speak. For example, you are unaware of all the bodily functions taking place continually for which the Subconscious Mind is responsible! You are breathing, your heart is beating, and when you have a reaction that you are not consciously aware of, your stomach churns, your throat tightens, and you may feel dizzy! So even though the Subconscious is truly running the show, the *Conscious Mind* is the only part you are aware of. That is the 'you' that you *think* is YOU. But it is really only about 0.00001% of you. The other 99.99999% of you—you don't really know!

The body is the link between the Conscious and Subconscious Mind. Remember that, as I am going to remind you of that a lot. It is important!

At first, when you start the CRV process, the Conscious Mind wants to do everything, answer all the questions, and feel real psychic right off the bat! Unfortunately, the Conscious Mind is NOT psychic, even though it wants to be. Sadly, the Conscious Mind is all EGO. Yup. It wants to be *right* all the time. It wants to be the *boss* all the time! And sometimes, under the guise of being *super helpful,* the Conscious Mind just keeps butting in, trying to guess what the target is, trying to tell you how to remote view, and trying to take everything over.

Lyn Buchanan used an analogy, called the President of the Company. It is rather long, so I am going to retell it here as my own abbreviated version. Lyn Buchanan's website has several wonderful analogies and their explanations. These analogies really help to convey the more abstract concepts within the field of remote viewing, and I highly recommend reading them. If you would like to read the complete Lyn Buchanan version, you can go to Lyn's website here: http://crviewer.com/analogies/analogy019.php

THE PRESIDENT OF
THE COMPANY ANALOGY

Imagine that you are the President of a company. This company has been your baby for many years. One day, the Chairman of the Board of Directors announces to you that he would like to train a young kid in the ways of being a company president, so he wants to allow the kid to run the company for a while.

Your first reaction is to feel threatened and territorial, right? After all, this is your company! But he is, technically, your boss, so you must comply. Imagine your surprise when the kid turns out to be your own son!

Now you are conflicted. You want your son to do well, but not too well! You begrudgingly hand over the keys to the company, but immediately, you begin to interfere. Every time your boy has a new idea, you tell him to shelve it until you are back in charge.

The Chairman sees the situation and sends you to the Bahamas to get you out of the way. But even on vacation, you can't relinquish control of the company! You are constantly on the phone to see what is going on, what is the boy doing now, etc.

Finally, the Chairman realizes there is only one strategy to really get you out of the way so the poor kid has a chance to try his wings. You are sent to the docks to get busy stacking boxes! Now you have a job to do, and you are being kept so busy with those boxes you no longer have time to interfere.

In this analogy, the President of the Company is your Conscious Mind. The boy is your Subconscious. When you begin a Controlled Remote Viewing session, your Conscious Mind will interfere constantly unless it is kept busy. How do we keep it busy? By using the very complex structure of CRV.

As you learn the structure, you may at times think, "Gee, this is really complex! Why don't they make it simpler?!!" Just remember that the complexity is intentional. It was developed *on purpose*. Why? Because if you simplify it, you make it easier for the President to regain control of 'the company'—i.e. the remote viewing session!

My students have become very familiar with this analogy, to the point that they frequently joke: "Oh, man, my President was all over this session! I couldn't get him to shut up!"

The President is in charge of **Logic**. He or she will constantly belittle perceptions, tell you they make no sense, and try to take over the session. But keeping your Conscious Mind busy remembering where to put things on the page is a wonderful way to make the Conscious Mind/President feel important! Let's give that President something to do!

Keeping this analogy in mind will help to clarify a lot of the reasons certain pitfalls come up as you are learning. No worries! Every discipline (and yes, CRV *is* a discipline) has its moments of frustration as you are learning.

You will learn to be patient and compassionate with yourself as you progress. It will take a while, but eventually, the sibling rivalry period passes. And when it does, you will discover that you have developed a deep friendship with yourself that will spread out into many areas of your life. What a reward for all that hard work!

Sometimes it helps if you think of CRV as an interview and report methodology. You can give the President yet another job in addition to stacking boxes at the docks! Allow the President/

Conscious Mind to be the reporter, or interviewer of the Subconscious Mind.

A reporter stays objective and detached and is focused on reporting the who, what, when, where, why, and how of his or her story, right? That is what your Conscious Mind will need to do.

As you progress, you will want to develop what I refer to as the 'objective observer', which is almost like having an external part of yourself that keeps an eye on what you are doing at all times and offers impartial, non-judgmental observations. This will come in very handy later on.

Now let's take a bird's eye view of the phases of Controlled Remote Viewing.

CHAPTER NINE:

THE PHASES OF
THE CRV STRUCTURE

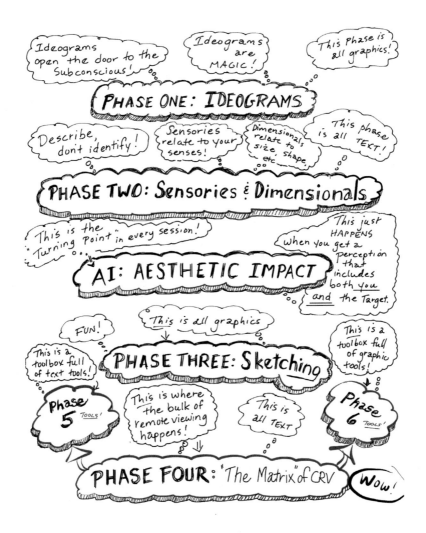

For many of us mere mortals, it really helps to have a framework of something we are about to learn so we know where we are headed. The structure of Controlled Remote Viewing consists of six stages, or *phases*, as we call them.

Phase 1

In Phase 1, we will learn all about *ideograms*. Ideograms are a graphic language for the subconscious mind. They allow your conscious mind and subconscious minds to communicate. In other words, *ideograms open the door to the subconscious!*

In a nutshell, ideograms are fast, subconscious squiggles or symbols that you will create with a spontaneous jerk of the hand. In the beginning, you will consciously form these shapes and then practice them until your subconscious mind learns them so well you can do them in your sleep.

Remember how you can drive for miles and not remember how you got home when you pull in your driveway? Just as your subconscious mind learned the way home, your subconscious mind will learn the ideograms you are going to create because you will practice them.

You'll be learning more about ideograms all throughout the CRV process. The subject of ideograms is an important aspect of the CRV process in all six of its phases. In the beginning, a lot of new Viewers just don't 'get' ideograms. Various instructors have different interpretations of how to work with ideograms during a remote viewing session.

Our ideogram method allows you to use ideograms in various aspects of your life. The specifics of how to use them daily comes further down the road of your remote viewing journey. For now, let's focus on the role of ideograms during Phase 1 of the CRV process.

In Phase 1, your initial ideograms will give you a quick snapshot of some of the major components at the target site. At first, these components consist of what we refer to as *gestalts*. The word *gestalt* is used in the CRV world as meaning *overall concept*. We begin the process by learning seven main gestalts: land, water, manmade, natural, space/air, biological/organic, and motion/energy.

Phase 2

In Phase 2, the Viewer begins to *describe* the target, using sensory and dimensional descriptors. Sensory words are words referring to sights, sounds, smells, tastes, touch and ambience. Dimensional words are words that have to do with shapes, sizes, patterns, positions and measures, etc. At some point in Phase 2, *something happens*. This mysterious 'something' is known as the *Aesthetic Impact*, or 'AI'. (See 'Aesthetic Impact' below.)

The Aesthetic Impact

The Aesthetic Impact happens when the Viewer has a perception that includes both him/herself *and* the target. This perception often (but not always) involves a sense of spatial relationship to something at the target site. The Viewer might say something like "It's taller *than me*" or *"I'm outdoors"* indicating an Aesthetic Impact. Strong emotions can also indicate that the Viewer is having an aesthetic impact. Once the Viewer has had an AI, the Viewer is officially in Phase 3.

Phase 3

Phase 3 is the sketching phase of CRV. However, the fact that a Viewer has had an AI and is 'officially' in Phase 3 does not mean the Viewer *has* to sketch.

Some Viewers are concerned about Phase 3 because they can't draw at all. But they needn't worry. There are many ways to use simple graphic techniques to obtain information about the target. In fact, some Viewers create what is known as 'Ideogrammic Sketches' in which they simply place their ideograms on a page, showing how the various ideograms relate to one another. During Phase 3, the Viewer may sketch, describe, sketch and describe alternately.

Phase 4

At some point during Phase 3, the Viewer may have a descriptive perception that is non-tangible, such as 'political' or 'touristy'. These perceptions are known as *conceptual perceptions* and are an indicator that the Viewer is now ready to move into Phase 4.

The purpose of Phase 4 is to remote view. In other words, Phase 4 is the phase of CRV in which the Advanced Viewer will do most of his/her viewing. Phase 4 is composed of eight or more columns, each with its own purpose. This set of columns is known as the Phase 4 Matrix. Phase 4 allows the Viewer to obtain an amazing amount of detail about the target site, including concepts, purposes, and even how a person or persons at the target site feel about something.

Phase 5

The purpose of Phase 5 is to provide the Viewer with a number of text-based tools with which to examine and/or break out the meaning behind nouns that have popped into the Viewer's session.

Our mantra is 'describe, don't identify'. When identifying words come to mind, they may feel very real to the Viewer but are often simply symbolic information about the target. While nouns are suspect and are often set aside (not to be taken literally), Phase 5 gives the Viewer the tools needed to break out the meaning behind the nouns that show up in session.

Phase 6

Phase 6 is another toolbox full of tools, like Phase 5, only much more extensive and based on graphics, rather than text. Phase 6 includes use of timelines, scalar lines, pendulums, rulers, modeling clay and toys with which the Viewer can build 3-D models of the target site.

Phase 6 allows the Viewer to obtain details that are not obtainable through other means, such as the height of someone, the actual dimensions of an object, the age of a person or a thing, when something occurred, and even the ideal time to take a certain action (like selling your stock, for example). These are just a few examples of the myriad uses for Phase 6 tools.

There are so many tools and such varied applications for these tools that we offer two separate three-day workshops to teach Phase 6! But not everyone *needs* both workshops. The second of these workshops teaches really advanced uses of the techniques, such as corporate strategic planning and is designed for students who want to become professional Remote Viewers in their own right.

BOUNDLESS: PHASE ONE

* * * * * * *

As you can see, the six phases of the Controlled Remote Viewing process are designed to allow anyone to obtain limitless information about anything in all of Time or Space!

CHAPTER TEN:

PREPARING FOR
THE STRUCTURE

At this point, you may be thinking, "Gee, the word 'structure' seems a bit overused in this book."

Ingo Swann, sometimes called the Father of Controlled Remote Viewing, used to have a huge sign over his desk that said:

SITE BE DAMNED! STRUCTURE IS <u>EVERYTHING</u>!!!

Ingo wanted his students to understand that 'getting the target' wasn't what they should focus on. Hoping they would grasp this elusive concept, he taught that by simply focusing on the structure of CRV, accuracy would naturally follow.

Notice that Ingo's sign used the word 'site'. The military Remote Viewers used this word to mean the location of the target, much in the same way it is used when referring to a landing site, for example.

The human brain is still a mystery, but certain things are known, and others are generally accepted. The first hemispherectomy showed the world that an entire half of a human brain can be removed, and the patient can function normally afterward if proper brain training takes place prior to the surgery.

But for the sake of *this* training, let's accept for now that the right side of your brain generally controls the left side of your body, and the left side of your brain generally controls the right side of your body.

As we get into the initial stages of the CRV protocol, in Phases 1 and 2, we are going to look at our paper as a representation of the human body. Right brain thoughts will be written on the left side of the paper, and left-brain thoughts will be written on the right side of the paper.

What? Isn't that confusing? It can be, in the beginning—until you get used to it. But remember, all of the CRV protocols were carefully created with the thought of keeping 'The President' busy. If nothing else, we keep the President busy trying to remember where to put things on the page.

If you think about it, the structure is really ingenious. By organizing our thoughts on the paper depending on where in the brain the thought originates (right or left side), we are effectively separating imagination from true intuitive perceptions! Once again, the drawer organizer comes to mind.

So grab a piece of paper, and let's try this out.

First, draw a vertical line down the center of your paper, dividing the paper in half.

Now your paper looks something like this (only much longer):

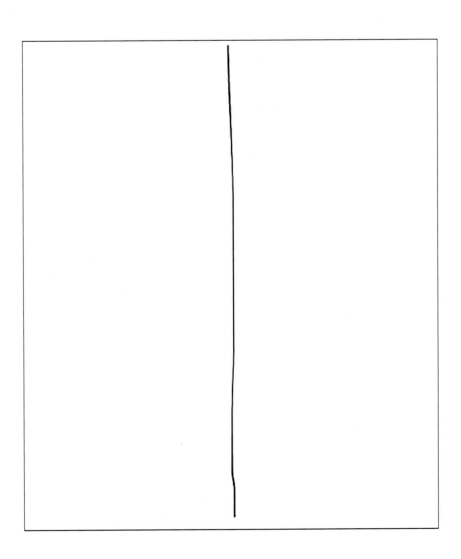

(When you start your real CRV session, you won't draw an actual physical line down the center of your paper, but I am using this as an illustration to show you how you will organize your thoughts.)

LEFT AND RIGHT BRAIN FUNCTIONS

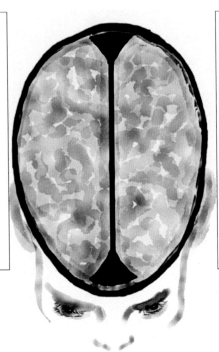

RIGHT BRAIN:

Art

Intuition

Psychic Ability

Creativity

Musical Talent

Imagination

Holistic Thoughts

Left Hand Control

LEFT BRAIN:

Analysis

Logic

Language

Reasoning

Science

Math

Writing/Spelling

Right Hand Control

If we take the above chart and adjust it for CRV purposes, it will look like this:

Psychic Perceptions	Administrative Information:
Words that DESCRIBE, rather than Identify: Adjectives describe nouns Adverbs describe verbs Prepositions (Examples: 'on top of' or 'behind')	Name Date Time Location Etc.
Sensory Words: Sounds Smells Tastes Colors Luminances Ambiences Textures Etc.	Notes about what is going on during the session or in your surroundings Nouns that come to mind Words that Identify, rather than Describe Names of People, Places or Things Full sentences or phrases Emotional reactions Physical issues or reactions
Dimensional Words: Shapes Sizes Patterns Positions Measures Etc.	Ideas about what the target might be Logic Analysis of any kind

GRAB A BLANK SHEET OF PAPER.

On your own piece of paper, label the left side of your page with 'Right Brain Functions' and label the right side of the page with 'Left Brain Functions'. Then list the functions as you see them listed above. Writing things down helps you to remember them. Now if this seems confusing in any way, rest assured that we are going to go over everything one step at a time. And you can proceed as slowly or as quickly as you like. You can also go over each section as many times as you need to.

Keep in mind that whenever you learn something new, your brain needs time to form new neural pathways. Once they are formed, what once seemed difficult is suddenly easy.

LEARNING TO DRIVE

In 1991, we returned to the United States after living for many years in South America. I had to learn to drive all over again, because I had stopped driving while we lived in foreign countries. Public transport was cheap, and there was no need to endanger others with my less-than-perfect driving skills, especially when there were few driving laws that anyone obeyed.

So, I found myself back in the U.S., re-learning to drive at 34 years old. As luck would have it, the only car we could afford was a stick shift! My then-husband was my long-suffering driving instructor. After an afternoon of tension, I remember stopping somewhere to use the bathroom.

As soon as I entered the bathroom, I burst into tears of frustration. A lovely older woman stepped out of one of the bathroom stalls and came up to me, concerned. "What's wrong, Sweetie?" she asked with a kind Texas drawl.

Sniffing, I blurted out, "I am trying to learn to drive a stick shift and it is so COMPLICATED!!! I'll never learn how to do it!"

"Sugar," she responded comfortingly, "A month from now, you'll remember this moment, and you'll laugh. You will be driving that stick shift without even thinking about it!"

And she was right. A month later, I remembered that scene in the bathroom and her words. And I laughed.

That is how you will be with the CRV structure. It will seem complicated at first, but then you will get it. As you practice, before you know it, you will do it without even thinking about it! Once again, remember all the times you've pulled in to your driveway and asked yourself, "How did I get here? I don't even remember driving the last few miles." That happens because your Subconscious Mind knows the way.

CHAPTER ELEVEN:

YOUR BODY IS THE LINK— CRV AS A PHYSICAL DISCIPLINE

When you learn to do something so well and so often that you can do it in your sleep, that means that the Subconscious Mind has learned it. We often get lost in thought when doing some rote activity that we do regularly, such as washing dishes or folding laundry.

When the geniuses that invented the CRV method of accessing intuition were trying to figure things out, they realized that the Subconscious Mind has access to that *Great Big Cosmic Database in the Sky*. Call it what you will, we seem to be part of a huge net of consciousness that is all interconnected. Everything that has ever happened in all of Time and Space is located in this net, and we are all plugged in to it.

If you can accept that last paragraph for the sake of learning CRV, then stay with me for a bit more as I explain how this works.

If the Subconscious Mind has access to all this information, how do we access it? How can the information get from Subconscious to Conscious?

This problem is *not* a psychic problem. It is not that we 'just aren't psychic enough'. The problem is that the Conscious Mind and the Subconscious Mind *do not speak the same language*.

Your mind is full of chatter and thoughts and perceptions all the time, right? But most of that chatter is coming from the Conscious Mind—the President. The President is always busy assessing your surroundings, identifying threats, keeping you safe, planning your next meal, charting your course, etc.

Meanwhile, the Subconscious mind doesn't speak in language. Nope, the Subconscious can't speak English, or French, or Spanish, or German. The only way the Subconscious mind can communicate is through physical reactions—such as when your throat tightens, or your stomach churns, and through overall concepts. We understand concepts such as love and hate, for example, and we can have an understanding of these ideas without even verbalizing their meaning.

So, when you pull into your driveway and realize that you drove the last few miles while your Conscious Mind was busy fuming over your daughter's new scumbag of a boyfriend, and that you had no *conscious* awareness of driving, that means that your Subconscious Mind went to work, controlling your body and getting you safely home.

Your body is the link between the Conscious and Subconscious! Both minds interact with the body constantly. You consciously move your body at will, but at the same time, your heart is beating, your lungs are breathing, and billions of processes are taking place without your conscious awareness!

If the body is the link, then any method we use to open the door for communication between the Conscious Mind and the Subconscious Mind must be *physical.*

Controlled Remote Viewing is a *physical* discipline. We engage the body in every aspect of the process. You use your hand to write on the paper. Every thought is spoken *out loud.* That engages your mouth, your throat, and your vocal chords—as well as your ears!

Placing the words on your paper in certain locations requires the Conscious Mind to stay very busy. This keeps the Conscious Mind out of the way, allowing the Subconscious Mind to have full sway.

All thoughts get written down. We have several 'mantras' in CRV, one of which is, WRITE IT DOWN! Every thought you think must come out of your mouth and make it onto the paper!

Believe it or not, the act of speaking *out loud*—actually *saying* every single thought that comes into your head and then writing it down—can be very challenging! Most of us were taught to 'sit there and shut up' or 'children should be seen and not heard', so speaking and writing in a constant stream of consciousness just doesn't come naturally. And that is okay. Like everything else in CRV, you'll get the hang of it, and soon it will become second nature.

When working true operational targets, the order in which perceptions are perceived can sometimes be important. For that reason, when my students are sitting in front of me and learning CRV for the first time, I continually remind them to *keep moving down the page*. Why? First, it is part of the physical discipline of CRV. Next, since the *subconscious* nature of CRV is of paramount importance, the order in which perceptions are perceived can be very significant. The only way to know the order that the words/thoughts/perceptions came to you, the Viewer, is if you *always move **down** the page*.

Since we are writing on both the left and right sides of the paper, moving down the page continually means that there will be **visual gaps** in the writing as we write a few lines on the right side of the page, for example, and then move across and down the page to write something on the left side of the page. It pains me to waste paper (I love trees, too!) but we must do it for the sake of structural purity and understanding of the process that is taking place in your head.

Some of my more electronically-inclined students do their sessions on an iPad Pro, tablet, laptop, or the new Remarkable Tablet to keep digital copies of all their sessions and to save trees. If it works for you, do it! I'm all for saving trees. But if you, like me, find that you are sensitive to electronics, you may find you are more comfortable using paper and pen. Again, do what suits you best.

Example:

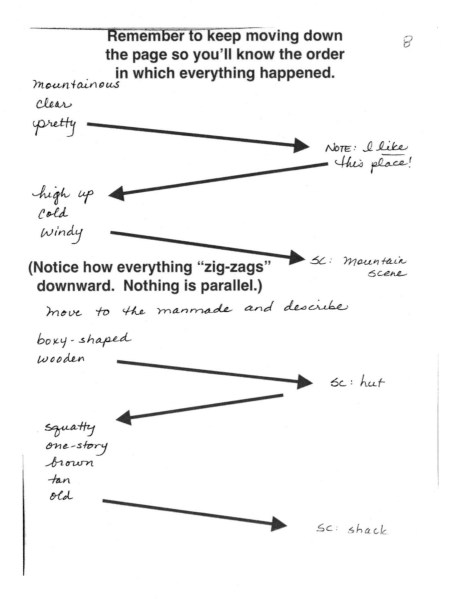

Notice how the writing is staggered **down the page?** None of the words in either column is parallel to words in the other column. That allows us to know the **order** in which the perceptions popped in. Make sense?

One more set of rules: If you are using physical paper, do not write on the back of the paper. And always use unlined white paper and a black gel pen. No pencils or erasers. No graph paper.

Okay! To wrap up this chapter, remember the two mantras you've learned thus far:

1. *Write it down.*

2. *Always move down the page.*

CHAPTER TWELVE:

DESCRIBE, DON'T IDENTIFY

Another rule of CRV that we might as well get out of the way right now is my personal favorite: *DESCRIBE, DON'T IDENTIFY*. This rule encompasses the main priority of Controlled Remote Viewing in a nutshell!

This mantra will come into play in Phases 2 and beyond. Why am I sharing it with you now? Because every new student will still attempt to name the target in Phase 1 and that will throw you off course. So, go ahead and learn the CRV mantra now. Memorize it and keep it on your fridge.

Why is *Describe, Don't Identify* a CRV mantra? We humans tend to grab nouns, or naming words, to identify things. But when it comes to CRV, we don't want to **name** the target. We want to **describe** it.

That can be an interesting challenge in the beginning because we are so addicted to nouns! When we were cavemen hiding in the primordial forest, our survival often depended on our ability to identify threats quickly and accurately: "Saber-toothed tiger! RUN!"

Let's say I have an envelope in my hand with a photo in it, and I ask you to describe the photo.

"Hmmm . . . let's see," you say thoughtfully. "It's something red, smooth, and shiny! I bet it's a red car!"

I hand you the envelope. You open it eagerly, sure that you will see a shiny new car sitting on the showroom floor just as you saw it so clearly in your mind's eye. As you slide the photo out of the envelope, to your dismay, you see a plump, ripe pomegranate. It is red. It is smooth. It is shiny. Your descriptors were accurate! Nevertheless, you are disappointed because it is not the car. As long as you were using adjectives—descriptive words—you were right! The minute you tried to name it, you went off track.

This scenario is the most common among first-day students in Basic class. Everyone wants to be a master psychic and name that target right off the bat. But that is not what remote viewing is all about. The goal is not to **name** it. This is not a 'guessing game'. I want to teach you to describe something so well that it will be very clear to the tasker (the person needing the information) exactly what the target is.

When it comes to remote viewing, most of today's CRV 'real world' applications require good, detailed descriptions of the target. This is where there is a difference between your average psychic and a good Controlled Remote Viewer. The psychic often feels very good when he or she *names* the target. When the police want some answers about where the murderer hid the murder weapon, and the psychic says triumphantly, "Oh, my GOD! He killed her with an AXE!" the police may react with, "Yeah, we know that! But *where* did he *put* the axe afterward?"

Or, what if the police need to know the location of the missing child, and the psychic says, "The missing child will be found under a bridge." Their response may be: "Wow, thanks a *lot*, lady—but there are fifty bridges in this city!!!" Sadly, not helpful.

Instead, a Controlled Remote Viewer would tell the police, "The target is underneath something structural, large, gray, cement-like, and arched, which is supported by multiple tall, white, cylindrical objects. On top of the structural gray thing are a lot of shiny, brass-colored cylindrical narrow pole-like things that have colorful flapping cloth-like attachments at the top."

The policeman in this example might react with "Oh, yeah! That is the Washington Street Bridge! The big gray bridge with a lot of international flagpoles on it," or whatever.

Addicted to Nouns

We grab nouns (rather than describing things) because:

a) we have formed that habit over years and

b) it is easier and shorter than describing.

But what are nouns? Besides being words that name things, nouns are (as Lyn Buchanan likes to say) 'boxes in which we hide things'. Each noun is like a gift bag, full of goodies! And every noun that comes to mind while you are remote viewing contains at least a kernel of truth within. But, along with that benefit comes the unfortunate truth that a lot of information gets lost when we grab a noun. And we sometimes grab a noun simply because it is less work than describing something more thoroughly.

So how do you break the noun habit and instead get used to describing things? The answers lie ahead in this class. Stick with me, here! At this point, you may be asking yourself, "What if I don't have a very extensive vocabulary? What if I have no idea how to describe things?" No worries! Like anything new, it is just a matter of learning to do it. There are simple steps involved.

Remember, any time you are learning something brand new, your brain must form new neural pathways. The more you practice, the easier it gets. Remember my story about me learning to drive a stick shift? You've got this, my friend!

Think about the last time you read a really good book, one that you just couldn't put down! J.K. Rowling's books about Harry Potter became very popular because she was so gifted at painting pictures with words. Good fiction writers are essentially artists who create vivid visual landscapes, using only words to describe them. So, one valuable tip for building a descriptive vocabulary is to read good fiction!

Now, if you feel intimidated or insecure at this point because you remember that you almost failed fifth grade grammar, don't despair! There are wonderful ways to boost this area. And a cool side effect of building your descriptive vocabulary is that you may actually raise your IQ and become more intelligent in the process!

Even if you are a grammar genius, you probably still have a noun-dependency that you have never been aware of until now. I've met very few people who don't have a dependency on nouns.

During my very first practice session, Lyn Buchanan interrupted me every two seconds to say, "That's a noun. That's a noun." for every word I spoke. And he was right! I constantly used nouns rather than describing the target. It was so frustrating! Then he began helping me to understand how to turn a noun into an adjective. For example, 'structure' becomes 'structural'. 'Metal' becomes 'metallic'.

A Quick Exercise

On the next page you'll find an easy exercise to help you break 'the noun habit'. Now, I know it is tempting to skip the exercises, but believe me, learning this *now* will help you *so* much when you move into Phase 2! So go ahead and give this exercise a try.

EXERCISE: CHANGING NAMING WORDS INTO DESCRIPTIVE WORDS

Instructions: Change the naming word on the left into a descriptive word on the right:

NAMING WORD:	DESCRIPTIVE WORD:
(Example Noun:) *Metal*	*(Example Answer:)* *Metallic*
Circle	
Wood	
Triangle	
Wool	
Colors	
Slice	
Wedge	

Fur	
Box	
Shine	
Light	
Pattern	
Stripe	

The Objective Observer

Since I am not there with you, watching you as you take your first steps into the CRV process, I can't correct every mistake. That means you will need to develop your own internal *objective observer* that helps you be more aware of what you are doing as you are doing it. This self-created objective observer will become more important as you delve deeper into remote viewing in the coming years.

What is an internal objective observer? Well, let me ask you this: Have you ever over-reacted to something? Maybe you were having a bad day, or ate some bad fish, or were experiencing PMS, and you picked a fight with someone you love. The next thing you know, you are yelling so loud and exerting so much energy, you feel as though you are going to burst every blood vessel in your face!

The objective observer is that still small voice of reason within. If you let it, it will guide you. It is like a calm inner friend asking, "Hmmm . . . do you think you might be overreacting?"

That is the wiser part of you, often referred to as the Higher Self. Pay attention to that still small voice of reason. As you develop your 'Remote Viewer' self during remote viewing sessions, that objective observer will be observing the pitch and tone of your voice, the twitching of your eyelid, the nervousness of your feet. It may ask you, for example, why your voice changed pitch right then. Was it because, on some level, you were reacting to something at the target?

This is just one example, but the idea here is that you want to start *paying attention.* Nothing is really a mistake. Anything and everything could be meaningful. A misspelled word in your session could end up being the answer! Don't underestimate the power of the subconscious mind to get its point across.

The Subconscious Mind Has its Own Personality

You'll discover that your subconscious mind has a personality all its own, with its own desires, sense of humor, and more! Therefore, as you begin diving into this process, try not to take yourself too seriously—at least not at this point. (I never like to take myself too seriously! Life is much more fun when I don't.)

You are just beginning the process of opening the lines of communication between your conscious and subconscious minds. Once that door is open, your subconscious mind may want to play! Puns, jokes, songs, famous quotes, clichés, and more may come to mind. They may or may not have anything to do with the target you are trying to view—but they are always meaningful.

Why does this happen? Your subconscious wants to establish a relationship with your conscious mind so that they can (eventually) form a dependable partnership—and that is a good thing! But the road to that partnership can be strewn with obstacles. While that can be frustrating, trust that it is just a part of the normal way things develop during your growth as a Remote Viewer. I can't protect you from this or keep it from happening any more than you can keep your 2-year-old and your 3-year-old from fighting with each other from time to time. It is just part of growing up! You just take a deep breath and push through it, knowing that one day, they will become the best of friends. It is okay.

Most of us find that the subconscious mind will play a lot in the beginning during practice sessions. But when you begin doing operational viewing—viewing for real people and on real cases—you will find that your subconscious knows the difference between practice and something truly serious or urgent. Practice sessions often give your 'Subbie' a chance to get to know you better or tell you something about yourself. But when push comes to shove and there is a life at stake, all the fooling around ceases, and the well-practiced subconscious mind will usually perform superbly.

Again, CRV is a martial art. With any martial art—in fact, with any true skill that you want to master—whether it is playing an instrument, learning tae kwon do, or developing exceptional psychic ability—you must practice a LOT and go through the pains of the ups and downs of growth. Figuratively, think of learning CRV as any other learning process—full of a lot of scraped knees, bruised egos, and sore muscles. You get the idea.

But the really *cool* thing about CRV is that—well, it's so *magical*! So even when you feel discouraged or frustrated, remember that you are pioneering the cutting edge of something that still holds so much mystery for most of the population. And the reward for all your effort is that you hold the keys to getting information to anything you have ever wondered about—in all of Time or Space! Who gets *that*? YOU do! Because you are one of the few who dare to step out of the mundane and believe in yourself. You are willing to challenge yourself to do more and be more.

What Is this 'Cutting Edge'?

It is Consciousness, itself. While this has become quite the buzzword and is overused, the truth is that very little is understood about how we, as humans, function. Did you know that there is more proven evidence that ESP, telepathy, and clairvoyance exist than that aspirin is effective against headaches?

Stanford Research Institute collected twenty years of evidence regarding our ability as humans to connect with each other, with events, locations, and more—via consciousness. The Food and Drug Administration has far less data to support the efficacy of aspirin as a pain reliever!

The very act of remote viewing with the CRV method will reveal a lot about you—your inner workings, thoughts, and opinions—some you didn't even know you had. While most of my students sign up to learn CRV with a specific goal in mind, the side benefits gained are too many to mention!

What Is a Monitor?

A CRV Monitor is someone who sits with the Viewer while the Viewer is remote viewing. The Monitor's job is to take care of the Viewer, study the Viewer's body language, and supply the Viewer's needs (water, food, break suggestions, etc.).

Good Monitors are hard to come by. Exploring a target thoroughly can also be made easier with a Monitor. Monitoring is discussed throughout the book.

Most of my students love working with a Monitor! To learn more about Monitoring, check out my book, *Monitoring: A Guide for Remote Viewing and Professional Intuitive Teams.* You can find a link to it on my home page: https://IntuitiveSpecialists.com or on Amazon.com.

Once you feel more comfortable with the structure, you can use the Monitoring guide to train someone to become your Monitor.

Here is a quick summary of the most important parts of this chapter:

1. *Describe, don't identify.*

2. *Work on turning nouns into adjectives.*

3. *Try describing more in your daily conversation.*

4. *Become more aware of how often you label things with nouns.*

5. *Create an objective observer!*

6. *Once you are comfortable with the structure of CRV, consider training a Monitor to be with you during your remote viewing sessions.*

MODULE II:

The First Steps of Your Remote Viewing Session

CHAPTER THIRTEEN:

PREPARING FOR YOUR CRV SESSION

Neural Pathways

On the first day of my three-day workshops, I let the students know that day one of Basic CRV may be the most difficult day of any remote viewing course I teach—EVER. Why? Because our brains need time to process information by creating neural pathways. As you learn the information contained in this course, be patient with yourself. If the information seems overwhelming at first, know that you are not stupid or slow—these are a lot of new thought processes! Give yourself time to grasp it. Each night as you sleep, your brain will go about the business of building the neural pathways you need, and the information will become easier and easier to understand.

The 'Cool Down'

If you have read any of the history books about the remote viewing military unit, you have probably heard of the 'Cool Down'. In preparation to remote view, each soldier had his own way of getting ready. One guy listened to heavy metal rock music. Another listened to Gospel. Some of the other 'cool downs' included listening to scriptures on tape, meditation, and even doing a set of chores in a row, so that the remote viewing was just another in a list of 'things to do today'.

Back when I first learned of the military cool down, I was heavily into exercise videos. Each one contained a 'cool down' at the *end* of the video—designed to cool your muscles after a hard workout. For that reason, the idea of 'cooling down' *before* doing something didn't make sense to me.

It might not make sense to you, either. But it wouldn't be right for me to teach you Controlled Remote Viewing without at least telling you about this important part of the process. You can call it whatever you want.

How do you know what your best 'cool down' method would be? For now, perhaps you won't know. You may need to document what your circumstances are before each practice session. For example, 'I just ate lunch' or 'I just meditated'. After you've done several sessions, you might start noticing a pattern developing. If you see that you are most accurate right after meditating, you might choose to meditate before every session as your cool down. You may be in a band and find out that you do your best sessions right after band practice. Each person is an individual, so try out a few things and see what works best for you!

I will talk more about the importance of establishing your own patterns during the Structure of the Administrative Section in the next chapter.

CHAPTER FOURTEEN:

INTRODUCTION TO THE ADMINISTRATIVE SECTION

As I mentioned earlier, I always like to prepare my students as though each one is going to become a professional Remote Viewer. Many of them have! Every detail is taught with that in mind.

As you prepare to begin your session, remember that good record keeping is essential. Every project and/or practice session needs to have certain information on the first page that lets you or anyone reading your transcript know which Viewer created it, the date on which the session was conducted, the time the session began, and other important data.

We are going to go over the parts that make up what is known as the Administrative Section of your session and why each part is necessary. Be sure to pay close attention to this. Often, a student may be tempted to ignore this part, but it really is essential that you learn it well. The reasons will be explained as we go along.

Here is what you will need to get started:

1. Clean blank white paper, free of lines or colors of any kind.

2. A black gel pen, such as the Pilot G-2 07.

We always use blank white paper without lines because we do not want any lines influencing the Viewer or the Viewer's sketches.

We talked about what to do if you hate wasting paper. For now, even if you love trees, do not use both sides of the paper. As I mentioned earlier, eventually you can switch to doing your sessions on an iPad, tablet, or tablet-type laptop. But for now, just grin and bear it and use paper and pen.

We use black gel pens because we often need to scan and email our sessions to a project manager or customer. Regular pens or pencils simply don't scan clearly.

Remember that the right side of the page is for the Left Brain. This is where we put anything analytical or logical, including notes, nouns, thoughts, ideas, and any recordkeeping—such as break times, resume times, etc. That is why we put the administrative information on the right side of the paper.

The Administrative Section is written in the upper right-hand section on Page 1 of your session transcript.

Speaking of Page 1: *Be sure to always number every page of your session.* Simply write the number in the uppermost right corner of every page. Believe me, if you ever do a professional session that is twenty pages long, and you accidentally drop the whole sheaf of papers on the floor, you will be glad those pages are numbered!

Here are the categories in the Admin Section:

Name/Viewer Number

Date

Time

Location

Monitor

Observers

P.O.C.A. *Preview of Coming Attractors*

P.O.C.D. *Preview of Coming Distractors*

S.A. Set Asides

Now let's go over each of these in detail:

Name or Viewer Number

The first thing you write in the Admin Section is your name. You can use just your first name, or your first and last name. For practice sessions that no one will see but you, it really doesn't matter. But for professionals, we actually use 3-digit numbers, known as Viewer Numbers.

The men in the military unit eventually were asked to choose three-digit numbers that they could use instead of their names. Of course, as spies, they all wanted 007!

The three-digit Viewer number can serve several purposes:

1. ***Protecting the Viewer's Identity***—Imagine that you have helped detectives catch a dangerous murderer. The detectives, thrilled with you and gleeful at having apprehended the criminal, just can't resist bragging to the criminal: "So-and-so, a professional Remote Viewer, saw you do it! She helped us catch you!" Kind of gives you the creeps, doesn't it? No one wants his or her name given to a dangerous person. Having a three-digit Viewer number helps the Viewer to remain anonymous in situations where it is preferable that no one knows you were involved in a certain project. So, remember that you can choose, depending on the circumstances, to either write your name or to write your Viewer number as the first thing in the Admin Section.

2. ***Data Base Organization***—Another aspect of the Viewer number is that it allows for better data keeping. Viewer numbers can be a quick way of knowing to whom certain projects have been assigned. That is a big help for the project manager or the database manager.

3. *Unique Coordinate Management:* To keep targets from getting all jumbled in what is known as Space-Time, each target chosen for remote viewing is given a unique set of numbers. These numbers serve as a sort of 'cosmic address' of the target and are called ***Coordinates.*** It can be important not to give the same number to two different targets. By assigning the same target number or coordinate to two different targets, you have essentially entangled the two targets together so that they are now one.

Let me give you an example. Let's say I am holding a red coffee cup in my hand and I say, "This is target 4567." I assign that to you as a target today. A year from now, I decide to give you a rusty bicycle as a target and I say, "This is target 4567." What *can* happen is that any Viewer assigned to view target 4567 will probably describe aspects of both the red coffee cup *and* the rusty bicycle. They have become entwined in Space-Time. (Remember the movie, *"The Fly"*? The guy gets his molecules entangled with that of a fly, and at the end of the movie, he has the body of a fly and the head of a human! Not a pretty picture.)

How to Create Your Own Viewer Number

Since this is a book, and I am not personally sitting with you and assigning you a unique number, I suggest that you **choose a three-digit number that begins with two numbers and ends with a letter of the alphabet.** So, for example, you could choose 58D as a number. Or, if you prefer, you can choose something that has meaning for you, such as your first two initials followed by a number. If your name is John Doe, you could choose JD1 as your Viewer number.

If you should ever study in person with me or another qualified teacher of CRV, you may be reassigned a Viewer number at that time. I use student Viewer numbers to keep track of how many students I have taught since I have been teaching under the umbrella of my own company. Other teachers may have a system of Viewer numbers that allows them to know which Viewers view on certain types of projects, etc.

If you prefer, the number you choose now can remain your personal Viewer number from now on.

Date

The next thing you write in the Admin Section (under your name and/or Viewer number) is the date. Depending on where you live, you may write day-month-year, year-month-day, or month-day-year. It doesn't matter in the Admin Section, as long as when you look at that session weeks, months, or even years later, you know when it was done.

Time

As this is a military discipline, we use military time. That is 24-hour time for those of you who are not accustomed to using it. From midnight to noon, time is the same for everyone: 1:00 a.m. for example. But as soon as noon arrives, you will add 12 to every number after that. So 1:00 p.m. becomes 1300 hours, 2:15 p.m. becomes 1415 hours, etc. If that is too confusing and you prefer to use a 12-hour format, go ahead. This is not an issue that will affect your development or accuracy.

Location and Circumstances

This is a great place to discuss patterns again. Patterns become an important tool for you to get to know yourself as a Remote Viewer.

Remember earlier when I talked about the 'Cool Down'? You might notice that you are more accurate when you remote view right after you meditate, or after a shower, or after a workout. Only by examining the target after you are finished with your session and scoring what you wrote down in your summary against what is really in the feedback photo will you know your patterns.

The same is true for locations, conditions, and emotions. After you have listed your name and/or Viewer number, the date and the time, you now want to list where you are viewing (such as 'my living room' or 'my bedroom', for example) and any conditions you want to note, such as 'just ate lunch' or 'just worked out'. Later, you may notice patterns that either lead you to greater accuracy or cause you to be not as accurate. I find that I don't view as well in the afternoon right after lunch, as I tend to feel lethargic and sleepy.

Years ago, I noticed that there were times of the month that PMS would cause me to feel nearly homicidal and other times I felt quite happy. I couldn't help but wonder which of these moods would produce greater psychic ability. I assumed that it would be when I was the happiest.

After keeping data for several months, I found out just the opposite: I was actually far more accurate when I was irritable and hormonal! Who knew?!!

Monitor's Name

You may not have the benefit of having a trained Monitor during your sessions. A Monitor was mandatory in the military, but modern Viewers rarely have the luxury of having a Monitor. (Refer to my book, *Monitoring: A Guide for Remote Viewing and Professional Intuitive Teams* to learn how you can easily train a monitor for your CRV sessions.)

If you do have a Monitor, you would list that person's name here. We do this simply because recording *all* the circumstances of a session can let you know, over time, how anything or anyone can possibly have an effect on the outcome of your viewing session. So, list the monitor's name here. If you do not have a monitor, just put 'No monitor' or 'NM'.

Observers

If you are doing a 'dog and pony show' or any kind of demonstration, be sure to list the names of any observers. Again, this is so you can see how you are affected. Performance anxiety can either work for you or against you. Performing under pressure, believe it or not, sometimes elicits an excellent response from the subconscious mind.

P.O.C.A.

This stands for **'Previews of Coming Attractors'**. Sometimes, right as you begin to do a session, you might have a sudden thought of what the target might be. For example, the thought, "I'll bet it's the Taj Mahal!" comes to mind.

Ingo Swann used to refer to this as an 'Advanced Visual', which would be noted with the acronym 'AV'. Lyn Buchanan changed this term to *Previews of Coming Attractors* because they are not always visual. It may have happened because you watched a program about the Taj Mahal on TV last night, and the TV show suddenly came to mind. Or, you may have just heard the words 'Taj Mahal' in your head. This idea (Taj Mahal) is then written down to be set aside later.

At this point, you may be wondering why we use *Previews of Coming Attractors* instead of *Previews of Coming Attrac**tions?***

Within the context of CRV, an *Attractor* is something at the target site that gets your attention. Let's say you just love anything that sparkles, and there is a beautiful crystal chandelier at the target. You may be so drawn to the chandelier, that you don't see anything else. You could miss the most important aspect(s) of the target, simply because the sparkliness of that chandelier is just so darned attractive.

Sometimes, that first inkling of what the target might be turns out to be right. But the fact that it is right is irrelevant. Our job as Remote Viewers is to describe, not identify. So just set it aside and move on.

P.O.C.D.

P.O.C.D. stands for **'Previews of Coming Distractors'**. Did you have an argument recently that has you gripped in its emotional talons and just won't allow you any peace of mind? I hate that! Things in our lives—little annoyances, duties, to do lists, etc.— have an amazing way of popping to mind just when we want to do a remote viewing session! You sit down to practice, and all of a sudden you think, "Did I pay the gas bill this month? I think I forgot. They may shut off the gas! I will freeze to death!" Or, you start to worry, "What if the dog wants out when I am in the middle of my session? What will I do?"

In 'CRV Lingo', a *Distractor* is anything in your life or environment that distracts you away from the intended target. So, a *Preview of a Coming Distractor* is anything that you anticipate could bother you during your session. (Note: Ingo Swann used the term 'Objectification' instead of P.O.C.D.)

We list both P.O.C.A.'s and P.O.C.D.'s in order to declare them so we can set them aside.

That leads us to the next (and last) item in the Admin Section: The Set Aside Process.

CHAPTER FIFTEEN:

THE SET ASIDE PROCESS

So how <u>do</u> we set aside bothersome things? We use a three-part method called *The Set Aside Process.* Believe it or not, in a live class, this is often the most difficult part of the class for people to really GET.

Why? Is it that difficult? No. People sometimes don't get it because they don't realize how important it is, so they gloss it over. Please, **don't gloss this over!**

If you do not learn to properly set things aside, they will hinder you on a subconscious (and sometimes even a conscious) level during the entire session!

My students tell me that the Set Aside process has helped them make it through tough times. A parent told me she taught the Set Aside process to her children and their grades improved because they could set aside test anxiety!

So please be sure to pay attention to this part, as it is crucial to having a successful outcome—and you can use it in other areas of your life. Ready? Here it is:

THE THREE STEPS OF
THE SET ASIDE PROCESS

Step 1: Talk about it.

Do you remember being a child? Did you ever have a nightmare? Let's imagine, for a moment, that you are a small child once again. You've woken up from a bad dream, convinced that there is a terrifying monster under your bed. You leap from the bed and run to your mother, screaming "Mommy! Mommy! There is a monster under my bed!!!!"

Your mother responds, "There is no damn monster! Get back to bed!"

How would her response affect your belief about the monster? Would you now be able to saunter confidently off to bed?

Of course not! But what if, instead of that impatient response, your mother was to very gently and lovingly guide you back to your bedroom where together, you both knelt and looked under the bed? Maybe she would even lie down with you for a while, to help you feel more secure.

This is the key to Step 1 of the Set Aside Process. You don't want your issues coming up while you are trying to remote view, so you must **state** what the issue is: "I am afraid of the monster under the bed."

Then, you **make a deal** with your subconscious mind to the effect of, "If you allow me to set this aside right now, I will go look under the bed as soon as my CRV session is over." Once the session is over, be sure to keep your promise!

Step 2

Step 2 is much easier: Just say the canned phrase "For now, I am not worrying about it." Easy, right?

Step 3

Step 3 is easy, too! Just say, "For now, I am setting aside the monster" and write 'monster' as you say it.

Of course, I am using the monster as an analogy. You will be setting aside whatever your issue may be, whether it is the fight you had with your partner yesterday, or the realization that you forgot to pay your gas bill again, or that your friend may call and interrupt your session. Whatever you think may come up while you are viewing, you will set aside at this point in the Admin Section. Get it out of the way so it won't haunt you during your viewing!

People often skimp on Step 1 and jump right to the setting aside part. They rush through it with something like, "I think there is a monster under the bed, but I am going to set that aside." Nope. That's not doing the set aside process. That is the equivalent of Mommy saying, "There is no damn monster. Get back to bed!" Your subconscious needs some cajoling, comfort, and reassurance. Or if you prefer, your subconscious wants to wheel and deal!

EXAMPLES OF A
TYPICAL SET ASIDE

Fear of Failure

(Step 1) "I am really worried that I won't be able to do this. What if I fail? This feels so crazy! And I'm not sure I really understand it.

But it is a learning process. My main focus should be on the structure, anyway. So even if I don't do as well as I would like, I'm sure I will get a lot out of it anyway."

(Step 2) "So for now, I am not worrying about it."

(Step 3) "For now, I am setting aside *fear of failure.*" (And write the words "fear of failure" **as you say them.**)

REMEMBER: Do NOT say, "I am afraid of failing but I am just going to set that aside." Go through all 3 steps. Be sure to discuss the issue, out loud, to yourself.

Argument

(Step 1) "I had that fight with Jane yesterday and it is really bothering me. I am worried that our friendship is over. She totally misunderstood what I was trying to say. But maybe she was having a bad day. I have those too, sometimes. She lost her job recently. I know! After my session, I will take some cookies over and see how she is doing."

(Step 2) "So for now, I am not worrying about it."

(Step 3) "For now, I am setting aside *argument.*" (And write 'argument' as you say it.)

Interruptions

(Step 1) "I am getting ready to do my session, but I'll just bet that the kids are going to wake up and need my attention, or the dog will want out, or something will happen to interrupt me. But if something does happen, I will just make a note that I am taking a break, and I can always resume my session later. That will be good for me, because I need practice in how to take breaks and how to work with distractions."

(Step 2) "So for now, I am not worrying about it."

(Step 3) "For now, I am setting aside *interruptions*." (And write 'interruptions' as you say it.)

Emotional Attractors

An Emotional Attractor is something at the target site that pulls your attention to it. If there is a strong emotional reaction to something at the target, that is noted as an "EA" or Emotional Attractor. Let's say you are claustrophobic, and the target is inside a very small cramped space. You may begin hyperventilating without realizing why. Remember my fear of heights mentioned in Module 1? The good news is that CRV can be a very safe way to overcome such fears.

Magic Words

In CRV, there are two words that have special meaning, and we refer to those two words as 'magic words'. I will talk about the second word a bit later. The first word is 'YES' and is used most often during the Set Aside Process.

Let's say that you are having an embarrassing physical reaction or physical condition that is bothering you. You don't want the world to know about it. Today, you happen to have guests who have been begging you to do a remote viewing session for them. As you do your set asides, you realize that you need to set aside your concern about this embarrassing physical condition, but you don't exactly want to announce it to everyone out loud. You can refer to whatever it is that you want to keep private as 'YES'. So, you would go through the three steps of the Set Aside Process, replacing the private issue with the word YES.

Let's use an example. Let's say you had beans and broccoli with fish for dinner and your intestines feel like a brass band has taken up residence inside, ready to blow at any minute! You don't want to state this, so you can handle it like this:

> (Step 1) – "I am concerned about YES. YES has been bothering me for a while, and I am uncomfortable. But I know I can go take care of it if needed, and as soon as my session is over, I will take something for it."
>
> (Step 2) – "So for now I am not worrying about it."
>
> (Step 3) – "For now, I am setting aside YES." (And write the word YES as you say it.)

Once you have completed the Set Aside process, you are done with the Admin Section of your session and ready to begin Phase 1.

You can bookmark the next page. It contains a template for you to use as you memorize the Admin Section structure.

CHAPTER SIXTEEN:

ADMINISTRATIVE SECTION TEMPLATE

The Admin Section belongs in the upper right-hand corner of Page One of your CRV Transcript.

NAME:

DATE:

TIME:

LOCATION:

CIRCUMSTANCES:

MONITOR'S NAME:

OBSERVERS PRESENT:

P.O.C.A.: *(Reminder: What you think the target might be. Any guesses or ideas you need to get out of your mind.)*

P.O.C.D.: *(Reminder: This is for anything that might bother you while you are in session. See example on the next page.)*

Set Asides: *(Reminder: Be sure to set aside both POCA's and POCD's. Use the 3-Step process.)*

On the next page you will find a handwritten example of what a completed Admin Section can look like. Yours will be different— based on your own circumstances, of course!

Lori
May 18, 2018
10:45 a.m.
Kitchen Table
Just worked out
m: Self
O: None
POC A: Taj Mahal
POC D: Dog
Phone Call
F.O.F.
Pay bills!
S.A: Taj Mahal
Dog
Phone Call
F.O.F.
Pay bills!

If this were a real remote viewing session, you would now be ready to move to the left side of the page and begin Phase 1.

MODULE III:

Moving into Phase 1

CHAPTER SEVENTEEN:
GETTING STARTED IN PHASE 1

As soon as you have finished your Set Asides, you are ready to move into Phase 1 of the CRV session. You will let your subconscious mind know that you are ready by moving your pen to the left side of the paper (the psychic, right-brained side, remember?) and you will *touch* the paper with the pen.

Once the tip of your pen has *made contact* with the paper, the monitor knows that you are ready to begin. If you don't have a monitor, touching the paper lets *you* know you are ready to begin. Always remember: If your pen is not making physical contact with the surface of the paper, your subconscious mind is not ready to begin the session.

Sometimes, without realizing it, my pen is hovering just barely above the surface of my paper. I think it is touching, but it isn't. My monitor will sit quietly. I am waiting for him to give me either frontloading or coordinates.

Finally, in exasperation, I will ask, "Are you going to give me my coordinates?" He will calmly respond, "Yes, as soon as you are ready." Then I look down and realize that my pen is still hovering in the air, not quite touching the paper.

When your pen *is* touching the paper, it is time to begin Phase 1. The first question that your monitor (or you, if you are self-monitoring) should always ask is, "Would you like Frontloading?"

NOTE: Frontloading of any kind does not make sense for Phase 1 targets. We only use frontloading in Phase 2 and 3. So for now, just read about frontloading so you can begin to familiarize yourself with CRV terminology in preparation for the upcoming phases.

115

CHAPTER EIGHTEEN:

FRONTLOADING: WHAT IS IT?

When a Remote Viewer is working a target completely blind, the target can be anything in all of Time and Space. If you think about eternity, well, that is a very, VERY LONG TIME! And all of *space*? That means anywhere in the Universe! Perhaps even other Universes or Dimensions! Who knows?

Amazingly, even with these daunting odds, many Remote Viewers zero in on the target time after time, with nothing more than the coordinate number. (For more information about coordinate numbers, see below.)

However, without frontloading, the Viewer could spend a lot of time and a lot of paper just 'getting on target'. Rather than waste the Viewer's time and energy, it can be helpful to give the Viewer some very neutral information before the viewing begins. This tidbit of information is known as *frontloading*.

There are those who strictly forbid frontloading, as they feel it is a form of pollution. They say, "Ingo never used frontloading!"

One of my students, author and psychic Debra Katz, has had the privilege of working through Ingo's papers stored in the archives at the University of Georgia. Debra gave a presentation at the combined Society of Scientific Exploration and International Remote Viewing Association conference held in Las Vegas in 2018.

To everyone's surprise, the remote viewing sessions for which Ingo is most famous—particularly his viewing of the planet Jupiter—were done completely frontloaded. Ingo *knew* what he would be viewing before his session ever started.

Yet, those who forbid it are correct: Frontloading *is* a form of pollution!

But here is how I feel about it: Life happens. There will be times when, in spite of your best efforts to protect yourself from getting any information about a target, you somehow overhear something, or someone rushes in and blurts out their emergency: "Help! Help! My dog just ran away! Help me find him!" You get the idea.

Remember, if you are not accustomed to receiving any information about the target, ever, you will be too delicate to handle this sort of 'pollution accident'.

The best Remote Viewers are versatile, tough and resilient. They can view anytime, anywhere, and under any circumstances. But how does a Viewer *become* versatile, tough, and resilient?

By occasionally getting just a little bit 'polluted' prior to viewing a target, the student Remote Viewer gradually becomes accustomed to having to work through pollution. Lyn Buchanan once created an exercise called 'Pollution Proofing' to help Viewers learn to work past the known information in order to 'go for the unknown'.

Once a Viewer has mastered the ability to look past all his or her preconceived ideas about the 'known' information, then nothing is too hard to view. A world-class Remote Viewer can work through anything and knows how to go beyond 'too much information' and instead go for the *unknown* aspects of the target. Then you, as the Viewer, have truly become boundless!

Again, if you want to become a really good, even *world-class* Remote Viewer, you must be versatile, tough, resilient, and able to handle pollution.

They say repetition is the law of memory, so let's go over this one more time:

What is 'Frontloading?'

Frontloading is when a Remote Viewer is given a small, **neutral** amount of information about the target before he or she begins to view.

Occasionally, a Viewer will begin a session completely blind to the target, but in the midst of the session, will decide to request frontloading. That is known as **mid-loading**.

And every now and then, a Viewer works through an entire session without any front or mid-loading, and just when the Viewer is ready to end the session, he or she will decide that it might be good to get some information just be sure that the question has been answered.

Frontloading given at nearly the end of a session is called **back loading**.

In any session, the first question you ask yourself (when self-monitoring) or that your monitor should ask you (if you have a monitor) is:

Would you like Frontloading?

You are the Viewer. You are in charge of your session. You can choose to accept Frontloading, or you can say, "No, thank you." When you refuse Frontloading, the next thing that will happen is that your Monitor (or you) will simply read the target coordinates out loud. You will write the coordinates down on the left side of the page exactly as they are being spoken.

As I mentioned above, frontloading is a form of pollution to the Viewer and if misused, it can ruin a session before it begins. So, let's establish a few simple rules to make sure that frontloading is helpful to you, the Viewer.

CHAPTER NINETEEN:
THE RULES OF FRONTLOADING

Frontloading must always be neutral

Frontloading must always be completely neutral. What do I mean by neutral? Neutral words don't necessarily contain a lot of stereotypes and they don't bring a lot of visual images to mind.

Let me give you an example of a word that is *not* neutral. Words that are not neutral are called *loaded words*.

Think about the word 'criminal'. If you, as a Remote Viewer, were asked to describe a *criminal* . . . what would you automatically come up with?

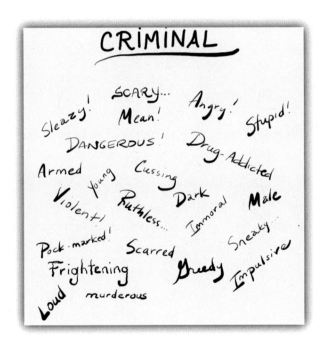

Remember: We ALL Have Subconscious Stereotypes

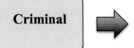

Criminal ➡ *Sleazy Mean Angry Dangerous Armed Pockmarked Male Violent Dark Drug-Addicted Sneaky Young Stupid Ethnic Loud Obnoxious Scarred Ruthless Immoral Smoking Cussing...*

You can see the variety of stereotypes many of us come up with automatically when we think of the loaded word 'criminal'.

Just imagine if you gave the police the list in the above box and it turned out that the 'criminal' in this case was the sweet little old lady who has been working for the company for fifty years and is the most trusted employee that no one would ever have suspected of embezzling! You can see how easily your information would lead the investigators astray.

The most important thing to keep in mind about frontloading is that it must be free of any loaded words, like 'criminal'.

Remember, loaded words are words that are laden with stereotypes and/or preconceived ideas.

How do we avoid loaded words?

Keep everything as neutral as possible. For example, exchange the word 'criminal' with something more general, such as 'person'.

We can neutralize any word that might lead the Viewer astray. This is a great thing to practice. Think of some loaded words and practice changing them into neutral words. Here are some examples:

LOADED WORD(s):	NEUTRAL EQUIVALENT:
Stripper	Person
Murderer	Person
Soccer Game	Activity
Parade	Event
Bombing	Event
Where is the body?	Location

Examples of the more 'generic' types of frontloading most commonly used:

The Target is manmade. Describe the Target.

The Target is biological. Describe the Target.

The Target is an event. Describe the Target.

The Target is an activity. Describe the Target.

The Target is a location. Describe the Target.

The Target is a person. Describe the Target.

When the second part of the frontloading is 'Describe the **target'** that means you can describe anything and everything you find at the target site.

For 'The Target is manmade. Describe the Target' you could describe the manmade items, objects or whatever, who is in or around the manmade thing(s), the time of day, the weather, what is happening to the manmade(s), and so forth.

For 'The Target is biological. Describe the Target' you could describe the biological element, what it is doing, its surroundings, the location, the lighting, the sounds, and any activities around it.

Now let's look at another way to phrase the 'generic' types of frontloading and what it can mean to the Viewer:

The Target is manmade. Describe the manmade.

The Target is biological. Describe the biological.

The Target is an event. Describe the event.

The Target is an activity. Describe the activity.

The Target is a location. Describe the location.

The Target is a person. Describe the person.

In these examples, the second half is more specific. This type of frontloading means 'just describe the one thing and nothing else'.

Why wouldn't everyone want the Viewer to take the opportunity to describe anything and everything at the target site?

Well, sometimes a very harried police detective just needs to know the color of the kidnapper's car. He doesn't want to know what the weather is like where the car happens to be parked. Perhaps he doesn't need to know who is in the car or even where the car is going. In this example, the policeman is the tasker, and he has a very specific need for very specific information. He doesn't want to wade through twenty pages of information to find that one thing he is looking for.

When a Viewer is able to focus on one tiny bit of information, we call that 'focused doorknobbing'.

Doorknobbing is a term that describes a situation in which the Viewer is so absorbed in describing one thing at the target, that he or she misses everything else.

This term came from a situation in which Lyn Buchanan was viewing a practice target in the military unit. Back in those days, they often sent someone out to a location and then instructed the Viewer to "view the location where So-and-so is right now."

For feedback, they would drive the Viewer to the location.

So, on this particular day, Lyn was describing something beautiful, transparent, faceted, cut like a diamond, and other details. He went on and on for about an hour.

When he finished up, he hopped into the car with his monitor and they drove out to the target site. It was a house, sitting on an empty lot. Lyn walked up onto the porch of the old wooden structure. There, he noticed the doorknob was made of crystal.

"There it is!" Lyn exclaimed. "That's what I was seeing!"

"Yes," said his Monitor quietly. "That is what you spent an hour describing. But the target was the *house*, not the *doorknob.*"

When doorknobbing happens unbidden, it can really screw up your session! And it can take some time for new Viewers to discipline themselves away from getting so absorbed by some fascinating, shiny thing at the target site that they stop viewing anything else.

Eventually, though, a well-trained Viewer will learn to doorknob *on purpose*. Being able to doorknob on the needed piece of information at will is a handy skill to develop.

Now let's ask ourselves something: Why are the examples above written in two sentences?

Any frontloading given to the Viewer must always be phrased in two parts.

Keep reading to find out why.

CHAPTER TWENTY:

THE TWO PARTS OF A WELL-FORMED QUESTION TO A VIEWER

Again, the following is not pertinent to Phase 1, but it is a necessary part of creating the foundation you will need for upcoming phases in the CRV process.

When we give any sort of directive to the person who is doing the remote viewing (including ourselves, when we are doing self-monitoring) we first ask the subconscious mind to do what we want it to do—and that is usually something that the conscious mind (aka: The President) *cannot* do.

That is why, when working with a Remote Viewer, it is helpful to give 'cues' or directives in **two** parts.

The first part is something for the subconscious mind to do.

For example, '*Move five hundred feet above the target*'.

You can't physically do that while sitting in your chair, working on your session, can you?

And what if the target is an event that took place eight hundred years ago? Your conscious, physical self certainly can't move to *that* target.

But your subconscious mind can easily do so. Isn't *that* exciting!

Again, we start the well-formed question by giving the Viewer's subconscious something to do.

Next, we want to follow that directive immediately with something for The President to do. For example, 'Describe what you see'. We don't want the conscious mind/President to feel left out. That's why we always follow up the directive to the subconscious by giving the conscious mind its own task: *Describe.* This second part can be 'Describe what you hear' or 'Describe what you see' or even just words such as 'sounds?' or 'taste?'

Adding this second part allows the Conscious mind to act as the reporter in this interview-and-report methodology that we call Controlled Remote Viewing.

In this example, the full cue would be:

"Move five hundred feet above the target and describe what you see."

Remember that the conscious mind acts as a reporter, so we want it to get busy recording everything that is going on.

In addition to frontloading, mid-loading or back-loading, you can use the two parts of a well-formed question to ask the Viewer to interact with the target or to move around the target.

We call the request to move around the target a *Movement Command.*

Movement Commands always begin with the magic word, '*move*'. We don't tell the Viewer to 'go' anywhere. We want the Viewer to *move* around the target site. Mentally moving from one thing to another at the target provides a great amount of information!

Examples of a Movement Command

Move twenty feet above the target and describe what you see.

Move forty minutes back in time at the target and describe.

Move to the most important aspect of this target and describe.

Move two inches away from the manmade and describe.

Examples of an Action Cue

We call the request to interact with the target an *Action Cue*.

Mentally slap the target. Density?

Mentally lick the target. Taste?

Clap your hands at the target and describe what you hear.

To review: Anytime you give an action cue or a movement command to a Viewer (even when that Viewer is you, because you are self-monitoring)

- Be sure to use both parts of the directive, remembering that

  a. The first part is a directive to the subconscious mind, knowing that it is able to go anywhere in all of Space and Time.

  b. The second part of the command is directed to the conscious mind, giving *it* something to do.

Now let's return to Phase 1.

CHAPTER TWENTY-ONE:

THE COORDINATE

When the military first began experimenting with CRV, they thought they had to have actual latitude and longitude. But then, situations began arising in which there were no known coordinates for the target. The target was in an unknown location. They discovered that the actual longitude and latitude was unnecessary—the Viewers were able to accurately describe the target without being given latitude and longitude.

Today's coordinates serve several purposes:

- Sometimes the target coordinate's numbers have meaning assigned by the Project Manager that allow the PM to know vital information about the session. For example, 'C22' may indicate the coded identity of the Viewer who viewed a particular target, '190418' lets the Project Manager know when—April 18, 2019 in this case—that target was assigned to a Viewer, and the number '25' could indicate the genre—archeological, law enforcement, corporate, scientific, etc.—in which the session belongs.

- When the numbers in the coordinate have an assigned meaning, that information can be stored in a database for important research projects. It is our hope that someday, this information will provide important data about how the subconscious mind works, how psychic and telepathic information is shared, and much more. This information can be a key to understanding consciousness more completely.

- Based on the current understanding of how these mysterious things work, the coordinates assigned to a specific target become that target's 'address' in Space-Time, allowing any viewer to tap right in to that specific target again and again, just by writing down the coordinate number.

- The simplest reason for having a target number is this: Writing down the number allows the Viewer's pen to be moving on the paper, creating the perfect opportunity for a spontaneous ideogram to appear! (*Reminder: An ideogram is a symbol that represents an overall concept.* You'll read all about ideograms in the coming pages.)

HOW TO FORM A COORDINATE FOR YOUR PRACTICE SESSIONS

Here is a simple way to create your own unique numbers for all of your practice sessions. If you have been given a six-digit number for a practice session, all you have to do is add your chosen three-digit Viewer number plus the numbers '011' to the coordinate assigned.

Then you will have two sets of six numbers, and they are placed to the left side of the page, with one set on top of the other, like this:

180221 < - *The first six numbers usually indicate the date someone created the target.*
56C011 < - *These six numbers make the coordinate unique to you.*

But what if a friend asks you to view something for him or her? How can you create your own practice coordinate? It is simple: Just use the current date backwards for the first set of six numbers.

If the year is 2019, for example, the first two numbers will be 19.

If it is the month of March, the second two numbers will be 03.

And if today is the 28th of the month, the last two numbers will be 28.

190328 becomes the first part of your coordinate.

Then, just as we did above, you will simply use your chosen three-digit viewer number for the next three numbers (example: 56C) and use "011" as the last three numbers.

56C011 will be the second set of six numbers.

**190328 < - *This is the date, written backwards: year, month, date.*
56C011 < - *This is your Viewer # and the "011."***

Remember that the last three numbers, '011' will usually always be '011' unless you happen to be doing two or three practice targets in one day (which I do not recommend). If you are on your second target of the day, for example, then your coordinate will end in '021'. If you were being really crazy and doing three targets in one day, that last target coordinate would end in '031'.

Once you get used to Phase 1, it can take five minutes or less to do a Phase 1 session. It is easy to do several per day, if you have the time. However, once you have moved into Phase 2, Phase 3 and beyond, I don't recommend doing more than one session per day. Why? This is a mental martial art and that at this point, your subconscious mind is like a child. It's easy to overwhelm a child with new experiences, so it's best to take it slow at first.

I remember when I was three or four years old; my parents enrolled me in ballet and tap-dancing classes. Every day, I was supposed to practice for fifteen minutes. FIFTEEN MINUTES!?! I thought I was going to DIE. Those fifteen minutes felt like FOREVER. I absolutely hated doing it. My beleaguered parents eventually gave up and pulled me out of class.

I don't want your CRV practice to become drudgery. Instead, make it fun for the subconscious mind. End on a high, reward the subconscious for practicing by doing something physically pleasant! Eat M&M's, take a bath, go for a walk or do whatever makes you really happy! And don't *over* practice!

To recap the formation of your practice coordinates, let's say that today, you are going to view one of the practice targets on my website, which you can find via this link: https://intuitivespecialists.com/target-pool/

You will simply choose one of the targets and write down the six numbers that correspond to that target like this:

080923

And then add your Viewer number combined with the number '011' like this:

56C011

Your coordinates will look like this:

080923
56C011

Why the '011' you ask? The '011' stands for 'This is my first target of the day'. The last '1' stands for 'This is my first time working on this target'.

So, if it is your *second* practice target of the day, you would put '021' instead, indicating with the '0*2*1' that 'this is my *second* target of the day' and again, that last '1' means 'this is my first time working on this target'.

Someone always asks, 'If I get up and go to the bathroom or take a week off in the middle of working a target, does the coordinate number change?' The answer is NO. Once you have established that number, it becomes like an address in Space-Time for *that particular target.*

While you are a student and just practicing, there really isn't a reason for the coordinate numbers to change once you have established them for a particular target. Only when you become a professional Viewer and are working on operational (aka 'real world') targets would you change those last three numbers—and that is just for database and record-keeping purposes that we don't need to go into now.

CREATING YOUR OWN
TARGET COORDINATES

Again, if you want to create your own targets, you can use the date backwards, like this:

190524 (which means 2019 — May — 24th)

And then (again) just add your chosen Viewer number (27B, for example) followed by '011' like this:

27B011

Your practice coordinates in this example would look like this:

190524
27B011

All coordinates for your practice sessions will be twelve digits long, and you will write them with six on top and six on the bottom as shown above.

HOW IMPORTANT IS
THE COORDINATE?

There are varying beliefs about the importance of the coordinate with regard to the target, and at present, there isn't enough data to show which belief is most likely to be true.

If we consider that the coordinate is the 'address' of the target in Space-Time—then it is pretty important! And we certainly want to avoid giving the same target number to two different targets for that reason. (That would be like having your mother-in-law move into your bedroom! —figuratively speaking, of course.)

For example, let's say someone gives you a practice target. The target is a baseball game, and the coordinate for that target is

123456
789011

For the sake of this example, let's say that a year later, someone else gives you a practice target. The target is a wedding, and for whatever reason, the coordinate for that target is also

123456
789011

What *can* happen is that these two targets (the baseball game and the wedding) now have the same 'address' in Space-Time, and therefore *they become* **one** *target*—which can wreak havoc with the viewing results.

The session summaries done a year apart may contain elements of both a baseball game *and* a wedding—like a weird baseball-themed wedding or a groom dressed like an umpire. You get the idea.

For the Viewer, the biggest importance of the coordinate is simply to get your pen moving so you can do an ideogram! Other than that, the database manager or anyone keeping data or doing research will certainly consider the coordinate of utmost importance for the information that the coordinate numbers contain.

What do I mean by that? A database manager can create database fields that will give him/her information about the target session and will allow him or her to accumulate important data.

HOW SHOULD THE COORDINATES BE READ OR DICTATED?

Sometimes, a Viewer has a helper during a session. This person has a number of duties, one of which is to dictate the coordinates to the Viewer. If the Viewer has no Monitor, that is okay. The Viewer will need to learn how to monitor her-or himself. (See Chapter 28: The Role of the Monitor in Phase 1)

When the Monitor reads the set of twelve numbers, how should he or she do it? (And this goes for you, too, Viewer, if you are monitoring yourself.)

The coordinates should be read at a normal pace, with a cadence or rhythm of every two numbers or every three numbers. You would read the following numbers with a short pause between every two numbers or every three numbers in the same way you pause when there is a comma in a sentence:

17, 07, 29, 27, B0, 11

You can do the same thing in groups of three:

170, 729, 27B, 011

The Monitor should watch the Viewer as he/she writes the numbers. And the Viewer should be paying attention to the voice of the Monitor and writing as the Monitor dictates.

That keeps the conscious mind focused on the pace of the writing rather than thinking about the ideogram or the target, allowing the subconscious mind to move the hand into an ideogram when the time is right.

WHAT IF I MESS IT UP?

Inevitably, while the Monitor is dictating the coordinates to you, you may write the coordinates incorrectly. Or, you may screw them up while you are reading them to yourself during self-monitoring. That's okay. Don't worry, you can simply write, 'Abort' next to the incorrect numbers and rewrite them below.

The same goes for when the Monitor reads the coordinates incorrectly. We all make mistakes. It is not a big deal. Again, just write 'Abort', move your pen directly below the area in which you just wrote the mistaken numbers and have the Monitor read them to you again as you write them down.

You should also abort when the ideogram you just created feels somewhat 'forced'. The ideogram should flow out spontaneously and quickly as a natural extension of the coordinates. Whenever you feel the urge to create an ideogram, even if the coordinates are not finished being dictated to you, just do it. If there is *any* hesitation between the coordinates and the creation of the ideogram, abort. That second of hesitation is an indicator that the President (your conscious mind) has taken over the session.

You have done an excellent job getting this far, and I am proud of you! In my opinion, learning the ins and outs of Phase 1 is the toughest part of the entire CRV process! So you are doing great! Hang in there with me through Phase 1 in the upcoming Module— you will be so glad you did! While it may seem complicated at first, it will become easier as we go along if you stick with it and don't give up.

Now we are going to move on and talk about the mysterious language that you are about to create so that your conscious mind and your subconscious mind can communicate more directly than they ever have! Strap on your seat belt and get ready! Here come the *IDEOGRAMS!*

MODULE IV:

Ideograms

CHAPTER TWENTY-TWO:

IDEOGRAMS AND THE LANGUAGE OF THE SUBCONSCIOUS MIND

What Is an Ideogram?

As I mentioned earlier, *an ideogram is a symbolic representation of an overall concept.*

What does that mean? Read on, and everything will become much clearer.

Help! We Need an Interpreter!

Your conscious mind and your subconscious mind have been cohabitating in the same body since the day you were born. Yet they do not speak the same language. In order to encourage the two minds to communicate with each other, we need an Interpreter. Where do we find one? Well, we have to look for the one thing that can communicate with both minds and speak both languages.

Examples from the Subconscious:

For most of us, our dreams are filled with symbols rather than literal images. They may seem disjointed or illogical. Dreams come from the subconscious mind. Again, how often have you pulled into your driveway only to wonder, "How did I get here?"

That happens because you are so deep in *conscious* thought that you are not even aware of driving those last few miles. Who is driving the car for you? Your *subconscious* mind takes over and brings you safely home. Right now, your lungs are breathing, your heart is beating, and a billion different processes are taking place in your body that you are not *consciously* controlling.

Examples from the Conscious

Yet, if I asked you to raise your right hand right now, you could easily do that *consciously*. You can consciously walk, run, drive, eat, and talk. Your conscious mind can allow you to solve a math problem, conduct a business negotiation involving complex monetary formulas, and plan a meal.

The Body Is the Link

What is the common denominator from the two examples above? Your BODY.

The *subconscious* mind can control the body, and the *conscious* mind can control it, too.

When you spaced out while driving, your *conscious* mind checked out and began thinking (for example) about where you and your partner would eat that evening, and your *subconscious* mind stepped in and took over your body, driving the well-known route back home. Your <u>body</u> is the link between conscious and subconscious minds. The body can communicate with both the conscious and the subconscious minds and both minds can control the body. That's right: your own body is the interpreter between conscious and subconscious minds.

Opening the Door to the Subconscious Mind

In order to get the two minds talking to each other, we need to open a door to the mysteries of the subconscious. Some folks in the field of psychology would argue that we should not call it 'subconscious'—but rather *unconscious.*

But there is no part of you or me that is UNconscious. We are *always* conscious, even when we are asleep!

The Limin

Some of our consciousness exists above what we call the 'Limin'. Imagine that the Limin is like a thick membrane stretched between your conscious and subconscious minds.

Everything above the Limin, where our conscious awareness lies, is 'super-liminal'. And some of our consciousness is rumbling away beneath the Limin and is 'subliminal'.

Just because it is below the Limin and therefore beneath your conscious awareness doesn't mean it isn't there. It is there, all right! In fact, probably 99% of the 'you' that you are—is beneath the Limin and you are not aware of it. And perhaps up to now, the only way the 'subconscious you' has been able to talk to the 'conscious you' is through dreams, aches and pains, and occasional flashes of insight.

No one can get *through* the Limin! It is too tough! We have to go *around* it. To open the door to the subconscious mind, we must get past the Limin—and there is only one way to do that: Through the

body. We are going to create a *physical* language that uses the body to communicate.

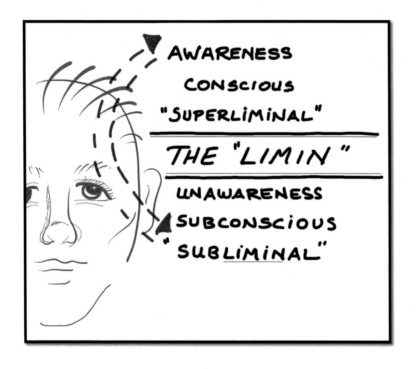

CHAPTER TWENTY-THREE:

CREATING THE LANGUAGE

To get these two minds talking to each other, we must create a physical language that both conscious and subconscious minds can comprehend. The conscious mind thinks in *words.* The subconscious mind relates through *concepts,* known (in CRV lingo, anyway) as *gestalts.* We already understand words and what words are. But before we can begin to create the language, we need to understand gestalts.

What are 'Gestalts'?

The official definition of the word *Gestalt* is *"an organized whole that is perceived as more than the sum of its parts".* In the CRV world, a gestalt is an overall concept. We begin with the following seven examples. You will use the seven gestalts listed below for all of your practice sessions for a while.

1. **WATER** – The word 'water' is a **noun**. A noun is **the name of a person, place or a thing.** When we think of water, an ocean or a lake might come to mind. But water comes in many forms: ice, raindrops, snow, steam, clouds. Even the wine in your glass or the sweat on your brow can fall into the *idea,* or *gestalt,* of water. So when you think of the *gestalt* of water, remember that we are not just talking about that clear liquid that comes out of your faucet. *Water* as a *gestalt* can be many things. However, it isn't just *liquid* because water can also be a gas or a solid.

2. **LAND** – Again, 'land' is a noun, right? But there are so many types of land! Dry land, marshy land, inclined land, sandy land, rocky land . . . well, you get the idea. Land can be mountainous or cratered, flat or hilly. Land can be lush or barren, deserted or crowded. The *gestalt* of land can be so many things!

3. **MANMADE** – 'Manmade' —as a gestalt—means anything that is created, constructed or conceived of by a human (or even an alien, I guess!). Buildings, vehicles, aircraft, hot air balloons, ships, boats, rockets, computers, clothing . . . I could go on and on. You can see how the gestalt of manmade, like land and water, is very broad and contains much more than just the simple noun 'manmade'.

4. **BIOLOGICAL** – Among CRV'ers, we use an abbreviation of 'bio/org' as a short way to write the gestalt of 'biological/organic/live'. This gestalt means anything that is living or has had life. Examples include trees, grass, people, dogs, cats, cockroaches, microorganisms, bacteria, silk made from silkworms, cotton, and anything else that is living or has had life.

5. **MOTION/ENERGY** – Most people consider 'motion' and 'energy' to be two separate things. But anything in motion exhibits energy, right? Sunlight is energy but if you look at the sun through special telescopes at an observatory, you see that the sun is always in motion. So for the sake of simplicity these two nouns are combined into one gestalt: motion/energy. This would encompass anything containing light, heat, and especially anything in motion—boy running, a cat playing with a string, laundry flapping on a clothesline, a car driving down the road. All of these (and much more!) would include the gestalt of *motion/energy.*

6. **SPACE/AIR** – This gestalt is among the simplest of our seven examples. Space and air are all around us. We

breathe it and we walk within it. It can be clean or dirty, high up or on the ground.

7. **NATURAL** – 'Natural' was one of the gestalts chosen by the 'Father of Remote Viewing,' Ingo Swann, but is often found to be the most confusing of the initial gestalts for beginning Viewers. Viewers think of 'grass' as being 'natural' —but it is also biological and organic. The overlap between things that are perceived as living and things that are natural seems at first glance to be redundant. Personally, I like 'natural' as a gestalt. To me, 'natural' means something that is not manmade but is not living, either. In my own viewing experience, whenever I come across 'natural' (and I will explain how that happens in just a few minutes), there is always something rock-like or made of stone at the target.

Ideograms as a Language for the Subconscious

We've established that your body is the link between your conscious and subconscious minds, and that the subconscious mind thinks in gestalts. And now we have set up seven simple gestalts with which we are going to begin the conversation.

Since the body is the link, the language we establish must be both gestaltic and physical in nature. Remember, CRV is a martial art, like karate or tae kwon do. Therefore, it is *physical.*

Let's Create Some Ideograms!

To begin creating this amazing language, we are going to create handwritten symbols to represent each of our seven gestalts. The rule of thumb is that each symbol must be as basic and simple as possible. Something you could do in your sleep, without thinking, as an instant gesture on the page. Here are the steps to follow:

- Grab some blank paper and a black gel pen.

- For this exercise and for all of your remote viewing from now on, make sure your paper has no lines on it. In other words, don't use lined notebook paper or graph paper. Just use ordinary typing or printer paper.

- Down the left side of the page, write the word 'WATER'.

- Next to the word 'WATER,' create a **symbol** that represents water. *Most Viewers make a simple wavy line. You can make yours as unique as you like but remember that **it has to be super simple!***

Did you do it? Great! You have just created your first ideogram! That wavy line (or whatever you created) represents the *gestalt* of 'water'. Good for you!

Don't worry about whether or not the ideograms you choose are 'right for you' or perfect enough. You can always change them later. In fact, as your subconscious and conscious minds develop a friendly relationship between them, you may find your well-practiced ideograms begin morphing. That is totally normal, and a part of the process.

To continue creating your ideograms, do just what you did for 'water'. Only this time, you will be creating a super simple symbol for the rest of the six words.

Here are some examples of what my ideograms look like for the seven example gestalts:

LAND

This is my ideogram for the gestalt of 'LAND'.
Most Viewers use a straight line.

WATER

A wavy line is my ideogram for the gestalt of 'WATER'.
Again, many Viewers use a wavy line for 'water'.

MANMADE

A right angle in various configurations is frequently used by many Viewers to represent the gestalt of 'MANMADE'.

BIOLOGICAL/ORGANIC/LIVE

An upward loop is my ideogram that represents the gestalt of 'BIOLOGICAL / ORGANIC / LIVE' — meaning anything living or that has had life.

MOTION/ENERGY

An upside-down 'U' shape is my ideogram that represents the gestalt of 'MOTION / ENERGY'.

SPACE/AIR

A big round circle is my ideogram for the gestalt of 'SPACE/AIR'. This ideogram might show up when something is very high in the air or in an aerial photo, for example.

NATURAL

A checkmark is my ideogram for the gestalt of 'NATURAL'. For some Viewers, the gestalt of 'NATURAL' seems to overlap with 'biological,' for example. But I like this gestalt. I find it appearing whenever rocks, stones or stonework is a prominent feature at the target.

While you are welcome to copy my ideograms as a starting point, please note that this is *your* language and can be totally unique to you. Eventually, as you grow and progress, you will find your ideograms morphing and changing. And as the relationship between your conscious and subconscious mind improves and becomes more of a partnership, the conversation becomes a two-way street! Your 'subbie' —as some Viewers like to call it—will begin giving your conscious mind ideograms, which will begin appearing spontaneously in your sessions! That is when things become very exciting! Learning the meaning of new symbols can become like a fun game, as you discover what your subconscious mind wants to communicate to you.

The following anecdote illustrates how the subconscious mind can supply new ideograms and new gestalts.

MEXICAN FLYING GYMNASTS

It was late evening, and I had finally finished all the duties that come with being a busy mom in a household full of children. The house had grown quiet. Finally, I could sit down at the little round table in the corner of my bedroom and do a practice session for this exciting new mental martial art I had only recently learned.

After completing the Admin Section on page one, I wrote the target coordinate number down as I read it out loud to myself. As soon as the last number was written, a very strange scribble formed spontaneously as my pen-holding hand jerked quickly several times.

Looking down, I saw that the scribble looked like a very complex knot, its lines twirling and twisting several times on top of each other.

"What could that be?" I wondered. Then I had to write down that thought, because I knew the instructions I had been given were very strict: Write everything down!

After completing the analytical process to examine the ideogram, I realized that I had no idea what the ideogram could be. It didn't look or feel like any of my seven practiced gestalts.

I went through Phases 1, 2, and 3 and finished by writing my summary. I had thought of a fan, a wind mill, something on a cylindrical base with a fanning out of something attached to the top of the base.

When I pulled the feedback photo out of the envelope, I was surprised to see a photograph of three men performing a ritual or ceremony in which they fall backward out of a basket attached to the top of a very tall pole. They are wrapped in ropes and use the musculature of their bodies to unwrap from the ropes in a controlled, graceful descent.

But this is not the end of the story. One full year later, I did another late-night practice session. After finishing my summary, I pulled out the feedback photo. To my surprise, I saw the same men, falling out of the basket.

"Hmmm . . . where have I seen these men before?" I wondered. I went to my files, where all of my sessions were neatly organized with target feedback photos on top of every completed session. Quickly, I located the session done a year earlier of the same men.

Shocked, I compared the ideograms on Page 1 of both sessions. Each one had an identical "knot" of an ideogram, as though I had traced over the original to create a copy! Thrilled, I realized that I had just experienced something special; my subconscious mind wanted to talk back to my conscious mind. A new ideogram had formed, but I had not consciously created it. It was a gift from my subconscious mind. An ideogram that to me means "something up in the air".

Ideograms Are a Language

When you were in kindergarten, you learned the alphabet. Thinking back to those days, remember how you were taught that the letter 'C' has a curved shape and can sound like 's' or 'k'?

Then you learned that the letter 'A' is shaped like a pyramid and can sound like 'aye' or 'ahh'.

Next, you may have learned that the letter 'T' is shaped like a pole with a roof on top and sounds like 't'.

When the teacher put these three letters on the board, you experienced the revelation that this particular combination of shapes and sounds represents a furry feline creature: CAT.

Why *is* that? Why do our English letters have both a *shape* and a *sound?* The letters we were taught in our early childhood are so ingrained in our psyche that we don't even think about it. That is where we are going in our study of Ideograms.

Shape + Feeling = Gestalt

Ideograms are a written language and are much like any other written language: The *shape* of the ideogram is not all there is! We also assign a *feeling* component to each ideogram.

When I say 'feeling,' I am referring to a tactile sense. Here are some examples:

**Rough. Smooth. Hard. Soft. Gritty.
Sandy. Sticky. Mushy. Bumpy. Slick.**

'What?!' you might be thinking. 'How can you **do** that?! How can a simple squiggle on a piece of paper have a *feeling*?'

How did the letter 'C' end up having both a *shape* and two *sounds*? Someone simply made that decision over a thousand years ago. A conscious choice was made. The English alphabet was born!

Let's say you've chosen a straight horizontal line to represent the gestalt of 'land'. The shape of the line is straight and horizontal but you also need to choose a feeling. You determine that a straight line that feels **hard** is your ideogram for the gestalt of land.

I will show you how this all works in a bit, but for now, simply choose a feeling for each of the shapes you chose above.

Here are some more complete examples:

(Shape): Straight horizontal line + (Feeling): Hard = LAND
(Shape): Wavy horizontal line + (Feeling): Soft = WATER
(Shape): Right angle + (Feeling): Smooth = MANMADE
(Shape): Upward loop + (Feeling): Slick = BIOLOGICAL
(Shape): Upside-down 'U' + (Feeling): Sticky = MOTION/ENERGY
(Shape): Circle + (Feeling): Fuzzy = SPACE/AIR
(Shape): Check mark + (Feeling): Rough = NATURAL

So now **you** will create your own language by making a set of ideograms that are composed of both a *shape* and a *feeling.*

NOTE: Keep in mind that the shapes and feelings you choose today are not set in stone. You can change them as needed. Most new students make their shapes too complex in the beginning.

Phase 1 Exercise

Below you will find a list of the seven beginning gestalts. Next to each one, draw the shape you have chosen. Next to that, list the tactile feeling that you are assigning to each one.

GESTALT:	IDEOGRAM (Shape)	IDEOGRAM (Feeling)
LAND		
WATER		
MANMADE		
BIOLOGICAL/ORGANIC		
MOTION/ENERGY		
SPACE/AIR		
NATURAL		

Simple, Compound, and Complex Ideograms

Just like grammar, ideograms may be simple, compound, or complex. A simple ideogram is just one gestalt, like land, for example. A compound ideogram is two or more ideograms combined. For example, a wavy line (water) connected to a straight line (land) could mean 'Land/Water interface'. A wavy line on top of a right angle could represent a manmade under water. A right angle on top of a wavy line could represent manmade over water. You get the idea. Look at some of the examples below:

Although these ideograms are contrived for the sake of this example, you can get an idea of what 'land/water interface' might look like.

160

This is what 'Water on top of Manmade' might look like.

'Manmade on top of Water' could look something like this.

161

This would be my ideogram for
'Bio/Organic connected to Manmade'

How to Practice with My Free Practice Program

Now it is time to teach your subconscious mind the ideograms you have chosen. This is the first step in opening the doors of communication!

To make things easier for you, a FREE Ideogram Practice Program is available on my website here: https://intuitivespecialists.com/ideogram-practice/

Follow the instructions on the website and begin your practice. The idea is to adjust the speed to your liking, and then simply write the symbol (ideogram) you create as the word (gestalt) is dictated by the program.

At first, it may seem awkward, because you aren't familiar with your ideograms just yet. But as you write, it will become easier and easier. I suggest that you start your practice by setting up the program to use just two ideograms to begin with—like 'land' and 'water'.

162

Once you are able to write the ideogram for each of those two without even thinking about it—you are ready to add another. Remember not to add another gestalt until you have learned the first ones so well that you can do them subconsciously. That means you find yourself writing the ideograms as the program reads them to you, but suddenly you realize that you have written several lines while you were spacing out and thinking of other things. That's when your subconscious has taken over and has learned the symbols.

Writing the ideograms while thinking about something else is a good indicator that your subconscious mind has learned them well. Congratulations! Keep going in this process until you have all seven ideograms memorized and can write several lines while your conscious mind drifts off, perhaps wondering if you remembered to pay your gas bill this month.

Practice once a day for only two to three minutes. That is about as long as it takes for your conscious mind to get bored and wander off, thinking about other things. The more familiar you become with your ideograms, the better the relationship between your conscious and subconscious minds will become.

Adding to Your Ideogram Vocabulary

Once those first seven gestalts are well-learned and practiced, you may want to add to your ideogram vocabulary. How do you do that? First, think about words you may need. Students sometimes ask me which words I added first. I created an ideogram for 'male' and one for 'female'. Why? Because I wanted my subconscious to be able to indicate to me whether humans at the target were male or female.

Here are just a few examples of common gestalts that some Viewers add to their ideogram vocabulary:

BIO/ORG	CONCEPTS:	MEDICAL/EMOTIONAL
Animal	Danger	Mental Illness
Human	Deception	Emotional Illness
Male	Political	Physical Illness
Female	Drug Addiction	Grieving

Remember, wait to add a new ideogram to your vocabulary until all the other ideograms you have are truly subconscious—so you could almost write them in your sleep! Think about pulling in your driveway and asking yourself how you got there. Your subconscious mind knows the way, right? THAT is how you should be with your 'learned' ideograms. You know them *so* well that you can have the ideogram practice program randomly saying the gestalts out loud while you absent-mindedly write out the symbols—all the while planning what you will have for dinner tonight.

* * * * * * *

At this point, you may still be trying to grasp why we use ideograms at all. When I first started learning CRV, my mentor regularly told me that the key to *everything* in Controlled Remote Viewing is based on ideograms.

"Ideograms are everywhere!" he often said.

At the time, I didn't understand what he meant. You know how sometimes you *think* you understand something but as life goes on you discover layer upon layer of meaning that you simply didn't see in the beginning?

That was how I was in *my* initial understanding of ideograms! As I used them, my understanding expanded. That will happen to you, too! So be patient. Know that they will become more meaningful to you as you use them.

Ideograms are MAGIC

Remember when I said that CRV is a *physical* discipline—a mental martial art? The reason it is physical is because *the body is the link* between the conscious and subconscious minds. That means that when you decide to move into Phase 2 (which we will talk about later), if you want to know more about a certain gestalt, all you have to do is **touch the ideogram** with your finger. That triggers the subconscious mind, letting it know that you are asking, "Tell me more about *this*".

Practicing Your Ideograms

Now you may be asking "How do I practice my ideograms?" or "How long do I practice?" or "How often should I practice?" These are all great questions!

First, remember that you will be working with those *first seven gestalts* I gave you in the exercise a few pages back.

As a reminder, they are **land, water, manmade, bio/organic, space/air, motion/energy and natural.**

Here is How to Find the Ideogram Practice Program

1. On my website at https://IntuitiveSpecialists.com, at the top of the Home page (which is where the website opens by default) you will see a tab that says, 'Free Stuff'. The link is here: https://intuitivespecialists.com/free-stuff/

2. Under the Free Stuff tab is a drop-down menu. Look for *Ideogram Practice.* Here is the link: https://intuitivespecialists.com/ideogram-practice/

3. When you first open the program, you'll see all seven gestalts. Start out by deleting all the words except 'land' and 'water'.

4. Control the speed by pushing the << or >> buttons. Set the speed at the fastest you can comfortably use.

5. Write the symbol (ideogram) as the gestalt word is spoken. Keep up with the speed of the voice as the words are randomly spoken.

6. Once you realize you have 'spaced out' and have written a line or two while busy thinking about something else, that is when you should quit for the day.

7. As soon as you can make the symbols without consciously thinking about it, you are ready to add another. Add 'manmade' for example. Then 'space/air'. Each time you realize that you are able to **unconsciously** make the ideograms as the program speaks the words to you, that means that your **sub**conscious mind has learned the ideograms! And that means you can add another word.

This exercise is designed to be about as boring as watching grass grow. The boredom factor allows the conscious mind to drift away, which is when the subconscious mind jumps in, takes over and learns the symbols. It should only take you two to five minutes a day to practice your ideograms!

When all seven gestalts are well-practiced, you are free to begin creating your own gestalts to suit your own needs!

CHAPTER TWENTY-FOUR:

USING IDEOGRAMS IN A CRV SESSION: PHASE/STAGE 1

The I — A — B Process

Now that you are more familiar with your ideograms and have (I hope) practiced them, it is time to incorporate them into your CRV session.

Where do the ideograms go and how do they work?

When you have completed the Admin Section of your session, you will move your pen back to the left side of the page, below the last line of your Set Asides, and you will put your pen on the paper. *(Remember, if the tip of your pen is not making contact with the paper, you are not ready to start yet!)*

If you have a Monitor, the Monitor will dictate the target coordinates to you, and you will write them as he/she reads them. But most new Viewers are working alone. If you are working alone, just read the coordinates out loud to yourself as you write them.

As you are writing the coordinates out, *as soon as you feel the urge*—allow your pen to do a spontaneous, reflex-type movement. I say 'as soon as you feel the urge' because that urge sometimes happens before you finish writing the full coordinates out. And that is okay! Allow it to happen when the urge strikes.

A naturally-formed (not consciously forced) ideogram will look like a scribble. This should be very spontaneous, like a knee-jerk reaction. If it feels at all forced or contrived, just write the word 'abort' next to the coordinate and start over by moving down the page and writing down the coordinates again, followed by another ideogram.

If there is *any* hesitation between the coordinates and the ideogram, abort and do it over. Why? Because in that second of hesitation, your President took over the session. The ideogram that follows that moment of hesitation is usually a very carefully drawn ideogram—created by your conscious mind. We don't want that! This is supposed to be a conversation with the **sub**conscious mind. So for that scribble to be a true ideogram, it must be completely subconscious. It should happen very quickly and spontaneously!

Once you feel you have a true, subconsciously created ideogram, you will look at it. Try to avoid the temptation to immediately label it. For example, some new Viewers look at the ideogram and say, "Oh! That's my ideogram for water!"

The reason I want you to wait to decide what that squiggly line represents is because ideograms are a new language that you are establishing with your subconscious mind. To get to know yourself and this amazing new language, we use a process to analyze the ideogram. Yes! Your conscious mind (the President!) must have a job to do, right? And analysis is definitely a left-brained activity— so it falls within the parameters of 'jobs I give to my President, so he/she won't feel threatened'.

What is this process?

We call it 'The I-A-B Process'.

The 'I' in the I-A-B Process stands for 'ideogram'. You have already done that part. But before we proceed to the 'A' part of the process, you need to *feel* the ideogram.

The first thing you will do when you look at the 'scribble' you just made is to *run your finger over it*. A few pages back, I introduced the idea that each ideogram not only has a *shape*, but also a *feeling*.

170

As you run your finger over the ideogram, try to sense a *tactile* feeling. Ask yourself, "How does this line *feel* under my finger?"

At this point, you may think I am nuts. "I don't feel anything! She is crazy! This is just a line on a piece of paper!"

True! It is just a line on a piece of paper, just as the letter 'C' is just a line on a piece of paper. Remember? We *assigned* the shape of the letter 'C' just as we *assigned* the sound it makes. 'C' doesn't really make a sound. But we *gave* it a sound, right?

That is how this works. You *assigned* a feeling component to each ideogram. But now, as you run your finger over that squiggle we call an ideogram, you are trying to see if you can feel a tangible difference in the line itself. You may notice that one part of the ideogram is sticky, for example, while another part is smooth.

As you run your finger over the line, see if you can feel any place where the line changes texture or feeling. If it does, put a small dissection mark where you notice the difference.

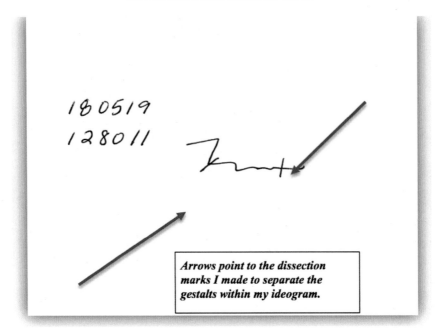

Arrows point to the dissection marks I made to separate the gestalts within my ideogram.

The act of lightly touching the ideogram and then moving your hand back to the spot in your session transcript where you are going to write the descriptive words that come to you tells your subconscious mind, *"I'd like to know more about the Manmade aspect of this target, please."*

Don't Linger!

Notice that I said, "lightly touch the ideogram". Why? When you are having a conversation with someone, do you do <u>all</u> the talking? What if you wanted to ask someone a question but you wouldn't shut up long enough for the person to give you an answer?

Imagine going into a coffee shop and asking the waiter, "Do you have any coffee? Because I LOVE COFFEE! I've been drinking coffee since I was eight years old! Yup! There is nuthin' like a good ol' cup of hot coffee! I want one right now! Got any? Cause I sure am thirsty for some coffee!" And on and on and on.

Meanwhile, the poor waiter doesn't want to be rude and walk away while you are talking, so he is unable to get you the coffee you so badly want—simply because you won't shut up!

In this analogy, if you keep your pen on the ideogram, tap-tap-tapping away, your subconscious mind can't answer you. You must bring your pen back to the place where you want to write the answers. That shows your subconscious mind that you expect and are ready for the answers.

You can be confident that your lightning-fast subconscious mind will have answers for you so fast, your hand can't even get to the spot before the information begins flowing again.

You may discover that you have only one ideogram, and that is fine. Or, you may feel that there are several places where the ideogram changes feeling/texture. Each place where it changes texture indicates a place where one ideogram stops, and a new ideogram begins.

Now that you have determined how many ideograms you have in that squiggle, it is time to analyze it. This is sort of like the moment when a child stares at the word 'cat' and has to sound out the letters to figure out the meaning of that particular combination of shapes and sounds.

As you continue, remember that the purpose of this process is to familiarize your conscious mind with the language that is being created. It may seem pointless at first, but trust me, it is a very important part of the process.

The 'A' Part of the I-A-B Process Has Two Parts

Motion. *The 'motion' component means the shape of the ideogram. This is where you describe the path your pen took on the* *paper when you spontaneously allowed yourself to do a quick scribble on the page. This will look like:*

Feeling. *The 'feeling' component means the tactile feeling of the ideogram. You will add the feeling component underneath the list of motions you just noted. For example*

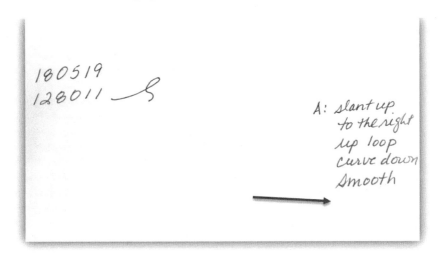

'B' — The WAG

'WAG' stands for 'Wild-Assed Guess'. That is just what the 'B' is for! Just take a wild guess as you look at your scribble. Compare your scribble with your practiced symbols. Which of your symbols do you see in that scribble?

In our continuing 'photo example,' when you have completed your *first* I-A-B process, it could look like this:

```
180519
128011   ⟋ₑ₇

                    A: slant up
                       to the right
                       up loop
                       curve down
                       smooth

                    B: Bio / Energy Motion
```

In the previous example, you may notice that my 'wild-assed guess' is a compound of 'Bio' and 'Energy-Motion'. While that particular compound ideogram could mean many things, let's say for this example that the target is a man, running a foot race.

It is very common to see more than one gestalt in your ideograms. 'Land connected to water,' for example. Or 'Bio on top of manmade'. You get the idea.

In the beginning, when I was a new student, my ideograms were generally single ideograms, such as 'Land' or 'Water'. But as I progressed in my understanding and practice of ideograms, compound ideograms, such as those mentioned in the paragraph above, began showing up.

Eventually, you may begin seeing complex ideograms, which are similar to compound ideograms, except that you might see three or more ideograms show up, separated by a space, as though your pen skipped across the page.

At this stage of the session, you should have at least one or more gestalts listed under the 'B' part of your session. The gestalts will be one or more of the following: Land, Water, Bio/Org, Space/Air, Motion/Energy, Manmade and/or Natural.

The I-A-B Process gives you an idea of the major concepts at the target.

Now that you understand the actual mechanics of Phase 1, let's talk about some of the reasons for this crazy phase.

CHAPTER TWENTY-FIVE:

THE PURPOSE OF PHASE 1

Phase 1 is all about getting in touch with the target. But we aren't really remote viewing yet—Phase 1 is all about the ideogram! Just to be sure you heard me, I have to ask . . .

Are We Remote Viewing in Phase 1?

The answer is: NO! Not yet!

(Sorry. I didn't mean to yell.)

The tendency for most new Viewers is to want to name the target right after they take the coordinates. Everyone wants to be the next Edgar Cayce!

Remember to focus on the *structure* of Phase 1. That is so important!

I once received a sample session from a student of Lyn's. Let's call him Mortimer. (Not his real name, thank God!)

Now, Mortimer had taken classes many years ago, and as often happens, his structure had morphed from what he had been taught in class. As I looked over his work, it appeared to be just a big jumble of words.

No ideograms. No I-A-B Process.

"Where is Phase 1?" I asked him.

"Oh," he said. "I never much cared for Phase 1, so I just leave it out."

WHAT???

**Phase 1 is the *foundation* of your *whole session!*
Without Phase 1, you do not have a session at all!**

Mortimer never became a good Remote Viewer because his sessions lacked the structure and foundation provided by Phase 1. All he could ever achieve was a few random perceptions—scattered about and virtually meaningless.

You see, we use the gestaltic information gained in Phase 1 to guide us into Phase 2, where we will move to each of those gestalts and describe them.

If there is no Phase 1—and therefore, no ideograms and no gestalts—how do you know where to go in Phase 2? What will you be describing?

Here is an example of how Phase 1 creates a foundation for the rest of your session:

Let's say that you took the coordinates and your first ideogram showed the gestalts of:

LAND   WATER   MANMADE   BIO/ORGANICE

When you move to Phase 2, you will move to the land and describe it. Then you will move to the water and describe that. Then you will move to the manmade and describe that. Then you will move to the Bio/Organic and describe that.

If my session words were a set of building blocks, it might look like this:

Brown	Blue	Metallic	Blond
Dry	Wet	Smooth	Feminine
Expansive	Vast	Green	Slender
Flat	Choppy	Horizontal	Young
Sandy	Salty	Moving	Well-dressed
LAND	**WATER**	**MANMADE**	**BIO/ORGANIC**

You can see that the **gestalts** you found in **Phase 1** created a firm foundation on which to build **descriptive information** gained in **Phase 2.**

To be clear: The above example is <u>not</u> an example of the structure of Phase 2, which we will cover in Book Two. This is just to give a graphic illustration of an imaginary foundation created by the gestalts we discover in our ideograms.

So please, whatever you do, don't give up on Phase 1.

When you consider the entire scope of Controlled Remote Viewing in its entirety, the concepts and practice of Phase 1 seem the most abstract. It is definitely the part of CRV that is the toughest to grasp. But I promise you, if you stick with Phase 1, you will find that ideograms can serve you in ways you can't imagine! They are the key to developing a good, solid, friendly partnership with your subconscious mind.

CHAPTER TWENTY-SIX:

THE 'FLOW' OF PHASE 1

In the beginning, working in Phase 1 just feels awkward! Everyone feels that way until they get used to it. So, no worries! Just dive in and give it a try.

At first, you are struggling to remember everything, so you stumble along, trying to get it right. That is the way it is with anything new! It can take a while to learn the structure and feel comfortable with it.

The goal is to become *fast*. Eventually, you will know what to do. Students who study with me in person feel pretty comfortable with the structure of Phase 1 by the beginning of the third day. Rest assured it won't take long.

Remember that when you slow down, it is usually because your President—the conscious mind—has taken over and wants to control the process. You will find that the conscious mind is very eager to 'help' —especially in the beginning—and will jump in before you even realize what is happening.

Your President will question everything you write down: "Are you sure? What if you are wrong?" And it will criticize: "That can't be right! How can it be both hot AND cold?"

The faster you can zip through Phase 1, the more *sub*conscious it will be—and the more accurate.

Now I encourage you to just practice Phase 1 until you feel comfortable with it. You can have someone choose magazine photos for you, or practice with my targets, which you can find here: https://intuitivespecialists.com/target-pool/

Focus on nailing *all* of the gestalts accurately. That practice will really pay off, as you will become very good at creating a thorough, accurate foundation each time you remote view.

To help you with the structure you have learned so far, you can use this template for the Admin Section and Phase 1:

Name:
Date:
Time:
Location:
Circumstances:
Monitor:
Observers:
P.O.C.A.:
P.O.C.D.:
S.A.

Coordinates and Ideogram
170916
---011

A: Motion
Feeling

B: Gestalt
(Wild-Assed Guess or WAG)

(Ask yourself, "There may be more gestalts at the site. Would you like to take the coordinates again?" Then continue taking the coordinates, doing the ideogram, the A (motion and feeling) and then the B [Gestalt or WAG] until you feel that you want to move into Phase 2.)

Coordinates and Ideogram

A: Motion
Feeling

B: Gestalt
(Wild-Assed Guess or WAG)

CHAPTER TWENTY-SEVEN:

PHASE 1 SESSIONS AND EXERCISES

Phase 1 is all about Gestalts. Accurately determining the gestalts of any target site helps create a solid foundation for the rest of your session in Phases 2 through 6.

While some gestalts, like "Natural" can be interpreted differently by different viewers, some are more generally accepted by all viewers.

Let's do a few exercises to see how gestalts can be interpreted.

How Many Gestalts Can You Find in this Photo?

Target #190209

List them here, in any order:

Did you find them all?

The answers are on the next page.

188

Here are the gestalts found in the target photo:

Land

Natural

Water

Biological/Organic/Live

Space/Air

Motion/Energy

How do these gestalts apply to the elements in the photo? (Learning this will help you learn how gestalts are categorized and determined.)

<u>LAND</u>: The gestalt of "Land" applies to the dry grassland in the picture. For most viewers, the mountains would also fall into this category.

<u>NATURAL</u>: The gestalt of "Natural" is the gestalt that is most nebulous for many viewers. As a viewer myself, my subconscious interpretation of "Natural" has proven to be anything made of stone or rock. But for some viewers, the mountains in this photo would be "natural."

<u>WATER</u>: The snow on the mountains and the barely-visible wispy clouds in the distance both fall under the gestalt of "Water."

<u>BIOLOGICAL/ORGANIC/LIVE</u>: The trees and dry grass fall under this category of gestalt, which is defined as "anything living or that has had life."

<u>SPACE/AIR</u>: The sky and air in this photo fall under this gestalt.

MOTION/ENERGY: While you may think there is no motion or energy in this still photo, your subconscious mind may think otherwise. With CRV, we are not teaching you to go to the photo. We are teaching you to view the **target.** The "default setting" for a target is usually the target site as it was at the time the feedback photo was taken. There are two ways the gestalt of motion/energy may be found at this target. At the time this photo was taken, there may have been a breeze blowing that is gently rustling the trees in the photo. And remember that *sunlight* is *energy.*

Not all viewers will pick up on all six of these gestalts. Some are less noticeable than others. As you develop your skills, your subconscious mind may only pick up gestalts that are noteworthy for one reason or another.

On the next page is an example of what a Phase 1 session and summary would look like for Target #190209. You will notice a few things in my session examples. For one thing, you will see the words "Session End" and the time noted twice.

Why?

In the military unit, they sometimes took a break between viewing and writing the summary. Nowadays, we try to avoid that because the Viewer loses that hot-contact with the target site. If you have to take a break or you get interrupted when you are about to begin writing your summary, go ahead and take the break. But when you come back, resume the session and do a few minutes of viewing to regain site contact before attempting to write a summary. That way, your subconscious is part of the summary-writing process. If you begin a summary cold, right after a break, it is often the President doing the writing! Remember, your President (the conscious mind) is *not* psychic.

A Phase 1 Session and Summary Example from Target 190209

Lori
Feb 9, 2019
13:18
Kitchen
(Just ate lunch)
M – self
O – none
POCA – Trees
POCD – I'm late!
FOF (Fear of Failure)
Tired
SA: Trees
Late
FOF

190209
127011 ①
②

A1: sweep up
loop
down
soft
B1: Bio/org
A2: curve
straight
across
hard
smooth
B2: Land

190209
127011 ①
②

A1: wavy across
soft
B1: water
A2: big up loop
smooth
B2: Space/air

190209
127011

① ② ②

A1 : Sweep up
over
down
fuzzy

B1 : motion/energy

A2 : down
sharp up
diagonal
slick

B2 : natural

Session End 13:29
Summary

The target contains elements of:

Bio/org
Land
Water
Space/air
motion/energy
natural

Session End 13:30

192

How Many Gestalts Can You Find in this Photo?

Target #190210

List them here, in any order:

Did you find them all?

The answers are on the next page.

Here are the gestalts found in the target photo:

Manmade

Land

Water

Biological/Organic/Live

Space/Air

Motion/Energy

Natural

How do these gestalts apply to the elements in the photo? (Again, learning this will help you learn how gestalts are categorized and determined.)

MANMADE: The gestalt of "Manmade" is found in the buildings and other non-natural elements in the photo: clothing, structures, bricks, windows, spires, etc.

LAND: The gestalt of "Land" applies to the cobblestone street. A viewer might find that his or her hand made a compound ideogram of "manmade-land" because the cobblestones are manmade, covering the land underneath. Indoor photos often prompt "manmade-land" ideograms because of the floor.

WATER: While difficult to see, there is a tiny bit of snow on the ground. (Hint: keep a magnifying glass around when you pull out your feedback photo for a closer examination of the target.) Additionally, the cloudy sky falls into the category of 'Water'.

BIOLOGICAL/ORGANIC/LIVE: There are several human beings walking around at this target. Any time there are people or animals at the target, they fall under the gestalt of

"Biological/Organic/Live." We usually abbreviate this long gestalt as: "BIO" or Bio/Org.

SPACE/AIR: The sky and air in this photo fall under this gestalt.

MOTION/ENERGY: People are walking. There may be a breeze, as it is early spring in Moscow, where this photo was taken.

NATURAL: The cobblestones are natural because they are made of stone.

On the next page is an example of what a Phase 1 session and summary would look like for Target #190210:

A Phase 1 Session and Summary Example from Target 190210

Lori
Feb 10, 2019
10:25
bedroom
recliner
after breakfast
M - self
O - none
POCA: bldgs
POCD: restless
FOF
appointmt
SA: bldgs
restless
FOF
appt

190210
127011

A1: aross
down
across
straight
smooth
B1: manmade/
land

190210
127011 ① ②

A1: wavy across
50 ft
B1: water
A2: up loop
fuzzy
B2: bio/org

196

LORI LAMBERT WILLIAMS

②

190210
127011

①
②

A1: big up loop
     soft
B1: space/air
A2: swoop
    sideways
    around
    back to left
    smooth
B2: motion/energy

190210
127011

⓪ ② ③ ④ ⑤ ⑥

A1: sweep up loop
    sticky
B1: bio in motion
A2: across & down
    smooth
B2: manmade
A3: down
    up
    over
B3: motion/energy
A4: side loop
    sharp corner
    down
    slick
B4: Bio
    manmade
A5: big down loop
    up & across
    bumpy
B5: space/air
A6: Across & up
B6: land/water

197

Session End 10:35

③

Summary
_____

The target contains elements of:

manmade / land
water
bio /organic
space /air
motion /energy
bio in motion
manmade

Session end 10:37

NOTES:

- Most of my ideograms are compound, meaning that they contain multiple gestalts.

- Ideograms can show up inverted, tipped on their sides, upside down, and misshapen. With practice, you will become comfortable and familiar with your ideograms. These small differences may eventually indicate something about the target.

- You may notice that my ideogram for 'space/air' and 'biological' look very much alike. I can tell the difference by the feel and the shape. 'Air/Space' is rounder than 'Biological' and tends to have a different tactile feel to it.

- As the Viewer, you have the right to add to, or edit your summary. While writing the summary, you may realize that the whole time you were in session, you "knew" there was water at the target, but perhaps you didn't get it as an ideogram. You can add it into your summary. But watch out! It is easy to begin making things up if you get carried away. We refer to that as "castle building."

- These examples are designed to show you the structure of a Phase 1 session. You can use them to guide you as you do your own sessions.

- Don't expect your sessions to be perfect.

  o Remember, you may not get *all* of the gestalts every time. That's okay.

  o If you get a gestalt that is not at the target, that's okay, too.

  o With every session, you learn something.

  o Each session is another opportunity for your conscious and subconscious minds to learn how to work together as partners.

  o There may be some squabbling between conscious and subconscious at first!

CHAPTER TWENTY-EIGHT:

THE ROLE OF THE MONITOR IN PHASE 1

What is a Monitor? In a remote viewing session, the Monitor is the person who sits with the Viewer and assists by providing assistance when the Viewer requests it. In more advanced sessions, the Monitor asks appropriate (non-leading questions) to get more information about the target from the Viewer.

Most new Viewers do not have the luxury of their very own Monitor. The thing so many Viewers forget is that *every session needs to be monitored* . . . so **you** must become your **own** monitor.

A few years ago, I realized that Viewers who learned to monitor themselves and others became much better Viewers!

Repeating everything you need to know about monitoring isn't in the scope of this book, so I really hope you decide to read the Monitoring book at some point.

For now, here are a few tips and pointers to remember:

- **The Viewer is always in charge of the session!**

- **Encourage the Viewer to move *quickly* through Phase 1.**

- **The Monitor can cue the Viewer through Phase 1, with cues such as**

- o "How many gestalts do you think you have here?"

- o "A: Shape? Feeling?"

- o "B: That is my ideogram for . . . _____."

Note that last one. The Monitor says "That is MY ideogram for _____" because he/she wants the Viewer to repeat those words exactly as the Monitor said them. The Monitor doesn't mean that it looks like the Monitor's ideogram. He or she just wants the Viewer to get into the habit of saying, "That's my ideogram for (blank)"—as saying it frequently helps impress that particular ideogram on the Viewer's mind.

CHAPTER TWENTY-NINE:

THE FOUR WAYS
TO GET OUT OF PHASE 1

Once you have taken the coordinates a few times, it is generally a good idea to move into Phase 2. However, there are actually four different reasons that a Viewer moves from Phase 1 into Phase 2, and here they are:

1) You are the Viewer. You just decide to move into Phase 2.

2) The gestalts begin repeating.

Example: Your first ideogram shows 'Water,' 'Land,' 'Manmade'. The second ideogram shows the same gestalts. It might be a good idea to move into Phase 2 at that point.

3) Phase 2 Descriptors begin bleeding into your Phase 1 work.

Example: You begin to have descriptive words, like 'blue' or 'educational' pop into your mind during Phase 1. List those as STRAY CATS on the right side of the page (you can abbreviate it as SC:) and prepare to move into Phase 2.

4) You get the ideogram with which you were tasked.

Example: Your frontloading was "The target is Manmade. Describe the Target." You have taken the coordinates at least once, and on the second or third time, the gestalt of 'Manmade' finally appears. That is an indicator that your subconscious is ready to examine the 'Manmade' aspect as you move into Phase 2.

CHAPTER THIRTY:

YOUR FIRST PHASE 1 SESSION

Now it is time for you to give this a try! Here are some online resources you can use:

Practice Exercises for Phase 1

Ideogram Practice link: https://intuitivespecialists.com/ideogram-practice/

Phase 1 Target Practice: https://intuitivespecialists.com/target-pool/

Instructions for Your First Phase 1 Session Assignment

- Begin your Phase 1 remote viewing session by completing the Admin Section as taught in Chapter 8.

- Once you have completed the Admin Section (including and especially the Set Asides!) you should move your pen across to the left side and slightly down the page.

- Make sure the tip of your pen is making contact with your paper.

- Write down the coordinate:

BOUNDLESS: PHASE ONE

- o   090817

- o   _ _ _ 011

- Be sure to write *your* Viewer number where the _ _ _ is in the coordinate above.

- Write the coordinate quickly and allow an ideogram 'squiggle' to naturally and spontaneously come from your pen as soon as you feel the urge to do so.

- As soon as you have written the coordinates and the ideogram, quickly *feel/touch* the ideogram with either your pen or your finger.

- How many gestalts do you think you have there?

- Be sure to go by the *feeling* of the ideogram, not by sight!

- Dissect the ideogram.

- Move to the right and slightly down the page.

- Write 'A:' and describe the motion your pen took as it formed the ideogram.

- Write the feeling you feel when you touch it. (Remember, it can't feel 'pink'. You are looking for a *tactile* feeling, like 'rough' or 'smooth'.

- Under that, write 'B:' and list your Wild-Assed Guess. Which of your seven gestalts showed up?

- If you like, you can repeat this process by writing down the coordinates again, doing another ideogram, and another A (motion, feeling) and B (Wild-Assed Guess).

- End the session by writing 'SESSION END' and annotate the time.

Now it is time to write a summary.

How to Write a Summary

Writing a summary for a simple Phase 1 target is very fast and easy!

- Just write the word 'SUMMARY' across the top of the page.

- Under that, write the phrase, "The Target contains elements of:"

- *List your gestalts in a vertical column down the page, on the left side.*

- The gestalts are your Wild-Assed Guesses (WAGs) that you wrote next to the B in your I-A-B Process.

- When you have listed the gestalts you found in Phase 1, simply write "SESSION END" again, and once more, annotate the time. We do it twice, simply because

  o It is helpful to have a record of how long it took to complete the session.

  o It is helpful to have a record of how long it took to complete the summary!

  o Writing 'Session End' reminds your subconscious mind that the session is over! The first rule of taking a break is *take a break!* Don't keep viewing!

Phase 1 Summary Example

Summary

The target contains elements of:

Land
Water
Manmade
Bio/Organic
Space/air
Motion/Energy

Session End: 15:34

Feedback and Scoring

Once you are done viewing, go to this link to see your feedback. Just push the feedback button:

https://intuitivespecialists.com/target/090817-2/

Next to each of your gestalts,

- Put a 'Y' for Yes (meaning you got it right!)

- Put an 'N' for No (meaning you got it wrong.)

- Put a '?' for anything you are unable to score. It may be there, it may not.

To Score Your Session

- Count all the possible answers.

- Then subtract any '?' —which are counted as 'un-scorable'.

- How many are Yes and how many are No?

- Divide the number of Y's by the total number of scorables.

- Then multiply that number by 100 to get the percentage of accuracy.

EXAMPLE: Let's say you had twenty-five total perceptions. Of those, you had five '?'. You subtract that five question marks from the number of total perceptions, leaving you with twenty scorable perceptions. 25 - 5 = 20

Of the twenty scorable perceptions, let's say you have five 'No's. That means you have fifteen Yes's. Divide the fifteen Yes's by the number of scorable perceptions, which in this example is twenty: $15/20 = .75 \times 100 = 75\%$

What did you learn from your first Phase 1 session?

CHAPTER THIRTY-ONE:

WHAT TO DO NEXT

Now that you have completed your first Phase 1 session, where do you go from here?

Practice! Practice! Practice!

The most important thing you can do is Practice! Practice! Practice!

Like any martial art or instrument you want to master, CRV requires practice. And all of us stay plenty busy these days! Believe me, I understand and sympathize. With seven kids, nieces and nephews, the additional teens we took in and my crazy job as the Director of Refugee Resettlement, I was as busy as anyone I have ever met when I began my remote viewing journey.

If you are as excited about exploring your consciousness as I have always been, you will be extra-determined to make time to practice. And soon, practicing Phase 1 targets will only take you about five minutes, including your summary!

How to Squeeze in Practice Time

- Keep a clipboard with paper attached to it with you at all times.

- If that is too cumbersome, keep a tablet and a stylus with you at all times.

- Keep a list of practice target coordinates from my website so you can copy the coordinate and look it up to get your feedback after you have completed your session and your summary.

- Utilize your small spaces of time to practice.

- I used to practice while I was:

    o waiting at the doctor's office

    o sitting in a park watching my kids play

    o at the airport

    o on a plane

    o a passenger in a car on a road trip

    o going on a walk in my neighborhood

Where and When to View

When I first began my CRV journey, I was a 39-year-old mother with a houseful of kids and a very demanding full-time job. I had to get all my practicing done "on the fly"—whenever and wherever I could.

To accomplish that, I always carried an envelope with a practice target in it along with some paper attached to a clipboard. That way, if I found myself watching the kids at the park, or in a waiting room at the dentist's office, or on a plane, I could whip out my clipboard and have at it!

This created a lot of versatility for me—being able to view at a moment's notice, anywhere and under any circumstances. Where there's a will, there's a way.

Once the kids were grown and gone, I had the ability to create a special spot in which to do my practice. For me, that was our small little motorhome, which we affectionately named "Ernie."

Ernie was a protected space for me. I felt safe in that enclosed box, with big windows and lots of light. I could spread my papers all over the dinette and no one would even realize I was inside.

One snowy winter night around 10 p.m., I received a call requesting urgent information through CRV. I had one hour to do the session and turn in the report. Jim and I were alone in the house, so I was surprised to see him putting on his coat and pulling on his boots—right over his red flannel nightshirt!

"What are you doing?" I asked.

"I'm going to go warm up the motorhome for you," Jim responded.

Even though I had the whole house available in which to view, Jim wanted to be sure I could view in the spot where I did my best work. So he willingly trudged through two feet of snow to warm up Ernie the Motorhome for me. What a guy! (Yeah, I know! I scored big time when I married this wonderful man!)

If nothing else, my story serves to let you know that you can view anytime, anywhere, regardless of the circumstances. Don't think you always have to have the perfect situation. Just do it.

On one hand, it is great to set up a place in your home that is your "spot" for remote viewing. This should be somewhere comfortable, with a good chair for you and if applicable, for your Monitor. A table or lap desk or TV tray would be good to use as a surface for your writing. Make sure you have water and even a snack nearby. This place should feel "just right" for you. As Lyn would say, give yourself permission to be psychic in this place.

On the other hand, you don't want to become *too* dependent on "your special place." It is great to have a special place to start your practice when you are a beginner, but don't let it become like a lucky rabbit's foot that you must have. You don't want to paint yourself in to a corner, where you think you cannot remote view unless you are in "your special place."

To keep that from happening, once you are comfortable with the structure, try practicing in a variety of locales. Try viewing at a bus station. Then try during your lunch break at work, or in a restaurant, an airport, on your front porch, in the bedroom, the bathroom (gross!), the basement, the living room, outside under a tree . . . you get the idea. Vary it up! Variety is the spice of life! And you will become an amazingly versatile Remote Viewer.

Find a Monitor—Someone to Practice With

A CRV Monitor is someone who sits with the Viewer while the Viewer is remote viewing. The Monitor's job is to take care of the Viewer, study the Viewer's body language, supply the Viewer's needs (water, food, suggest breaks, etc.).

Good Monitors are hard to come by. Exploring a target thoroughly can also be made easier with a Monitor. Most of my students love working with a Monitor!

Once you feel more comfortable with the structure, you can use the Monitoring guide to train someone to become your Monitor and/or to learn how to monitor your own sessions when working alone.

Moving into Phase 2 and Beyond

Once you feel comfortable with Phase 1 (or P1, as we often call it), it is time to move on to Phase 2. If you bought the complete Basic set, now is the time to pick up the second book in the series and dive in! Take your time. Be sure you understand one section before moving on to another.

If you haven't yet purchased the next book, now may be the time to do so, IF you feel that CRV is something you will enjoy and/or something you will be able to use to make a difference in your life, your work, your career, your loved ones, or (best of all) on this amazing planet.

If you would like to take the full Basic CRV course, you can take a live 3-day workshop with me by checking out the calendar on our website at https://intuitivespecialists.com/events/

If you are interested in learning more or just checking out what a video course might be like, here is a link to a FREE 4-part introduction to Practical Remote Viewing, or PRV. To access the free course, sign up here:

https://intuitivespecialists.com/masterclass-series-introduction/

We also offer a fun 6-week video course that you can take at your leisure. If you are interested in taking the full 6-week course, you can read all about it here:

https://intuitivespecialists.com/practical-remote-viewing/

This is the same information contained in my live CRV Basic course, but just in a format that allows you to study the full course on your own schedule, as your time permits.

Once you have taken either the 3-day Basic CRV workshop or the 6-week Video PRV course, you will receive a free one-month membership in the amazing online Club CRV!

In the club, you will receive weekly content from me, and will have access to recorded trainings, a private community located within our own Kajabi platform (no Facebook!), CRV session demonstrations, bonus materials, mentoring meetings, and once-a-month live Q&A sessions.

Why the Club? You take the course to learn the structure. You join the club to gain *Mastery*. Being part of a vital community of like-minded folks *inspires* you to *practice*, and it keeps you motivated, learning, and excited about your new skill!

Congratulations!

Congratulations for completing Book One of *Boundless: Your How-To Guide to Practical Remote Viewing!* This is really an accomplishment and I am proud of you!

Practice what you have learned so far until you feel comfortable with getting the correct gestalts for 20 practice targets. Then you are ready to move into Phase 2: Describing the Target!

I'll see you in the next class!

Reviews help authors like me so much. If you liked my book, would you do me a favor and write a review on Amazon.com? Positive reviews will lead others to read the book, too. My hope and dream is for people to discover their own amazing abilities and by becoming friends with themselves, to lift the Consciousness of the entire planet.

Thank you! ~ Lori Williams

APPENDIX A – RESOURCES

Recommended Reading:

The Seventh Sense
by Lyn Buchanan

The Essential Guide to Remote Viewing: The Secret Military Remote Perception Skill
by Paul H. Smith.

Remote Viewing: The Secret History of America's Psychic Spies
by Jim Schnabel

Mind Trek
by Joe McMoneagle

Monitoring: A Guide for Remote Viewing and Professional Intuitive Teams
by Lori Williams

When Things Fall Apart: Heart Advice for Difficult Times
by Pema Chodron

8 Martinis – A Remote Viewing magazine by Daz Smith – (Free Online!)

Recommended Movies

The Arrival – with Amy Adams

Interstellar – with Matthew McConaughey

Inception – with Leonardo DiCaprio

Recommended CRV Target Pools:

https://intuitivespecialists.com/target-pool/

http://www.crviewer.com/targets/targetindex.php

Websites:

https://IntuitiveSpecialists.com

www.CRViewer.com

ACKNOWLEDGEMENTS

Producing a book that attempts to teach the complex skill of Controlled Remote Viewing has not been an easy task. How does one take something so abstract and put it on paper in a way that will allow anyone to grasp the finer nuances of this amazing martial art? Teaching is my passion, and it has been a joy to take on this difficult task.

I want to thank my mentor, Lyn Buchanan, for the many years he patiently taught me. Lyn, you are one of a kind. Your excellent teaching skills, integrity and generosity have been a wonderful example for me to follow.

I owe a huge debt of gratitude to Jim Williams, Aleah Harrow and Shera Dalin for the many hours of editing and proof reading. Go, team! Thank you for all you do for me.

Many thanks to Tad Browne, Nathalie Bentolila, Dino Russo and Thomas Schumpert for your wonderful critiques of the book in its early stages. You made the book so much better with your suggestions and by letting me know of the areas that were not clear enough.

Mel Riley, thank you for our many phone conversations and the warm visits to your beautiful home. Jim and I cherish our friendship. There are many times I would have quit if not for you talking me through those dark nights of the soul.

To my students, who inspire me daily: If I could claim a super power, I would have to say that it is attracting amazing people like you. You are all so fun, supportive and hardworking! And your enthusiasm for CRV knows no bounds. I am blessed to have you all in my life.

BOUNDLESS: PHASE ONE

To the members of my Mastermind Operational Group: You know who you are. Thanks for years of amazing dedication, attendance to our meetings, and encouragement through thick and thin. You all are a huge motivator for me to continue this work. I love you all.

A special thank you to Aleah Harrow: Aleah, I couldn't have done this without your support! You make everything so much easier! Thanks for your dedication and sacrifices to help me daily.

And to the Love of My Life, Jim Williams: Babe, I won the lottery when you came into my world. I couldn't teach or write books or create blogs or videos without you by my side. You make me breakfast, get me to rest when I am over doing it, and provide me with hugs and snuggles and great advice when I need it most. And you cheerfully put up with me working around the clock to fulfil this mysterious destiny that drives me. Thanks for your sacrifice and demonstrating your love to me constantly. I love you.

ABOUT THE AUTHOR

Lori Lambert Williams was born in Spokane, Washington in 1957 to Darrel and Kathy Holt. Always filled with a spirit of adventure and wanting to know more about the unexplained, Lori spent her adolescence exploring books about the supernatural, paranormal and her favorite: ghosts!

In 1971, after meeting a group of Jesus People in a park, Lori spent the next 20 years exploring Christianity and eventually lived in South America from 1982 to 1991, where she became fluent in Spanish and fell in love with the Latin people.

Returning to the States in August of 1991, Lori called a wrong number and became a social worker with the Department of Human Services in Amarillo, Texas. Five years later, she became the Director of Refugee Resettlement with Catholic Family Service, Inc.

In 1996, Lori met Lyn Buchanan, and while still running the refugee program, began her passion for remote viewing in all of its forms. Knowing she wanted to teach, she traveled back and forth between Amarillo, Texas and Alamogordo, New Mexico for several years, apprenticing with Lyn in order to be able to one day teach his courses.

Lori is married to Jim Williams, a retired forensic scientist and skilled Reiki Master. Between them, they have nine children and twenty-one grandchildren.

LEGAL CAVEAT

DISCLAIMER

The information in this manual is intended to provide a skill set to the reader. This information must be practiced regularly in order to produce results, and even then, results are not guaranteed. Lori Lambert Williams and Lambert Williams Enterprises make no claims regarding the content in the book, or that the reader will make money or have an improved life experience by practicing the techniques described within this book. While to-date, there is no evidence that learning and practicing Controlled Remote Viewing is in any way unhealthy or dangerous, the reader/purchaser of this book/course assumes any and all risks associated with the practice of the techniques taught herein.

Made in the USA
Las Vegas, NV
07 June 2022

49926646R00143